T0229702

Reverse Design
Super Mario World

Reverse Design Series

Author
Patrick Holleman

Series Titles

Reverse Design
Super Mario World

Patrick Holleman

CRC Press
Taylor & Francis Group
Boca Raton London New York

CRC Press is an imprint of the
Taylor & Francis Group, an **informa** business

CRC Press
Taylor & Francis Group
6000 Broken Sound Parkway NW, Suite 300
Boca Raton, FL 33487-2742

© 2019 by Taylor & Francis Group, LLC
CRC Press is an imprint of Taylor & Francis Group, an Informa business

No claim to original U.S. Government works

Printed on acid-free paper

International Standard Book Number-13: 978-1-138-32325-4 (Paperback)
978-1-138-32326-1 (Hardback)

Library of Congress Cataloging-in-Publication Data

Names: Holleman, Patrick, author.
Title: Reverse design : Super Mario World / Patrick Holleman.
Description: Boca Raton : Taylor & Francis, 2018.
Identifiers: LCCN 2018022561| ISBN 9781138323254 (pbk. : alk. paper) |
ISBN 9781138323261 (hardback : alk. paper)
Subjects: LCSH: Super Mario Bros. (Game) | Video games--Design.
Classification: LCC GV1469.35.S96 H65 2018 | DDC 794.8--dc23
LC record available at https://lccn.loc.gov/2018022561

Visit the Taylor & Francis Web site at
http://www.taylorandfrancis.com

and the CRC Press Web site at
http://www.crcpress.com

Contents

Introduction

This is the third entry in the *Reverse Design* series. The goal of this series has been to reverse-engineer all of the design decisions that went into classic videogames. Of the other books in this series, the best companion for this one is the book on *Half-Life*, as it shares many design structures with *Super Mario World*. The other books are all on RPGs and work much differently than this one does. The books on *Final Fantasy VI*, *Diablo II,* and *Final Fantasy VII* are much more focused on game systems rather than level content. Because of that, it's possible to sit down and read those books, in order, in a few sittings. This book is longer than those books, and probably cannot be read straight through. Rather, the best way to approach this book is to read the first three chapters as one block, and then read the rest as you play each level of the game.

One of the driving motivations behind this series was the notion that we might learn more about videogame design by studying an individual game than by studying "videogames" in general. During the writing of this book, I saw an article about level design on a popular games industry website. Its major points included tips like "level design should be efficient" and "good level design is driven by your game's mechanics," with general explanations of what those points mean. Both points are great, but they're not especially helpful to anyone who hasn't already been designing levels for a long time. Although that article offers high-level principles about level design, it doesn't answer questions like "what do I put in level two?" or "how do I keep level three from being too much like level five while still keeping them similar?" Nor does it answer any of the dozens (or even hundreds) specific *little* problems that a designer will encounter while building a game. This book aims to explain how Nintendo answered the big questions and the little questions in *Super Mario World*. In doing so, it finds a method that can be applied to almost any kind of videogame.

When I looked at the way that levels are constructed in *Super Mario World*, I found a pattern. Following that pattern not only makes it possible to fill levels with content more easily, but it also makes it easier to make a game that is coherent, fair and fun. This pattern exhibits three levels of ascending complexity: the *challenge, the cadence, and the skill theme*. Those things are defined later in this book, because in order to understand them, one must first understand *Super Mario World*'s place in game design history. The challenge, cadence, and skill theme would not be possible were it not for the development of *composite games*. We're going to look at all of those ideas briefly in this introduction, and then in much greater depth in the sections that follow.

It's probably worth giving you a look at what the all of those things are, however, so that you can determine whether or not this book will be useful to you. The level design of Donut Plains 3 illustrates the key concepts of *Super Mario World*'s level design well. Below are several screenshots of various challenges in the level. Be warned: there's a lot of jargon coming, but you don't need to understand it yet. The example below is just meant to show where this book is going.

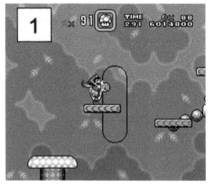

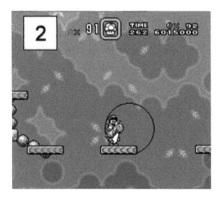

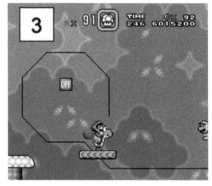

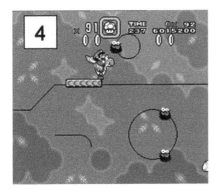 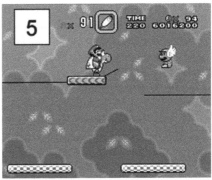

In order, these are screenshots of the standard challenge, an evolution of the standard challenge, an expansion of that evolution, an evolution of the first evolution, a divergent evolution, and an evolution/expansion that combines elements of two challenges. That's not all of the challenges in the level, but that's the important line of development. Essentially, this is a two-part "fork cadence" level that divides into two sections. One of those sections is based on platforms that move in loops, and the other is based on platforms that move along lines. We can extract the important data from this level by charting it in two different ways.

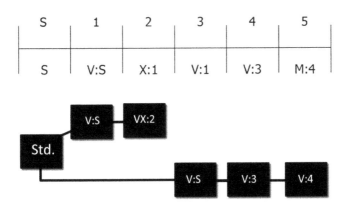

These diagrams are two different forms of what I call a *cadence analysis*. The last thing to know about the level is that it belongs to the "moving targets" skill theme. I know that was a lot of jargon, but don't worry if you didn't understand it all.

The first step to understanding everything that was going on in the previous paragraph is to begin at the beginning in 1981. That was the year that Shigeru Miyamoto, the creator of Mario, began his career as a game designer. Over the next few years, Miyamoto and his team created not just a game franchise, but an

---

entirely new method for designing videogames. The *Mario* series represents the bridge from the original arcade style of videogame design to the new "composite" style of videogames that he invented. Composite games became the dominant school of game design from 1985 until about 1998. Chapter 1 of this document will comprehensively define what composite games are. The short version is this: composite games combine two or more genres in a specific way to achieve (and maintain) a form of psychological flow. Haphazardly mashing two genres together doesn't work, but Miyamoto and his team figured out numerous techniques that allow different genres to play together in compelling ways. Game designers at different studios all around the world saw Nintendo's breakthrough and started using composite design techniques immediately, and with great success. A huge variety of games—everything from *Mega-Man* to *Portal*, from *Doom* to *Katamari Damacy*—are composite games. Early Mario games were always on the cutting edge: virtually every Mario title between 1985 and 1996 saw a significant advance in the practice of composite design. *Super Mario World* is no exception, and throughout this document there are frequent references to how the gameplay uses composite design techniques to keep the player entertained.

There is one last proviso that needs to be said here. Although I have found numerous patterns in *Super Mario World* and the history of videogame design as a whole, it is not my opinion that designers intentionally planned all of these things. In fact, Shigeru Miyamoto himself has admitted that for all of his best games, he and his design team tried a huge number of different design ideas, and simply kept the ideas that worked the best. Therefore, my opinion is that composite game design is merely a natural evolutionary step in the development of videogames. Composite design techniques worked well, and so designers kept using them, even if they didn't fully understand why they worked. It's likely that game designers have gradually become more conscious of the nature of composite design and composite flow, but proving this point would take a much larger study than the one being attempted here. It is enough to say that *Super Mario World* is a great example of the Mario developers taking their design techniques to the next level. This book explains how they did it.

Composite Games and the Historical Context of *Super Mario World*

Our first step in studying *Super Mario World* is to understand the game's historical context. The *Mario* series, though it seems safe and conservative now, began a revolutionary trend in videogame design. Before 1985, videogames were generally designed according to one central principle, what I call *Nishikado motion*. Nishikado motion describes the way that difficulty in a mainstream videogame rises and falls in a regular fashion. The phenomenon is named for Tomohiro Nishikado, who discovered it (serendipitously) in his masterwork, *Space Invaders* (1978). In that game, the enemy aliens start the level by moving slowly, and then get progressively faster before resetting with a slight uptick in difficulty when the next level begins.

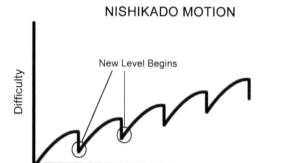

NISHIKADO MOTION

The graph above visualizes Nishikado motion as it occurs in *Space Invaders* and thousands of other games. This kind of ebb and flow in game difficulty is still, to this day, the central principle of videogame design. That said, videogames have evolved a lot since then. In the arcade era, designers achieved Nishikado motion through control over one or two variables. For example, Space Invaders gets harder when the enemies get faster. In *Asteroids* (1979), the game gets more difficult when there are more asteroids on screen, and those asteroids move faster. Most arcade games operated similarly.

Aside from Nishikado motion, the only other major development in the arcade era was the invention of the powerup. At first, powerups were little more than a way to push the difficulty of a game up or down. For example, the famous two-ships powerup in *Galaga* (1981) doubles the player's firepower, and results in a concomitant decrease in difficulty. In *Pac-Man* (1980), the benefits conveyed by the "energizer" powerup make the game easier for a few moments, but the length of the powerup's effect gradually decays across the course of the game. These powerups were fun, but they were really just back doors into control of the difficulty.

The first powerup to radically change videogame design was the invention of a young Shigeru Miyamoto. *Donkey Kong* (1981), in which Mario first appears (as "Jump Man"), opened a different evolutionary path for powerups. The hammer powerup in Donkey Kong doesn't simply enhance Jump Man's abilities quantitatively, it changes their nature qualitatively. When he obtains the hammer, Jump Man loses his jumping and climbing abilities and gains the ability to attack enemies with a weapon. Essentially, the game temporarily stops being a platformer and starts being an action game. The game does not abandon Nishikado motion; rather, it adds to it. We can visualize it like so:

1. Composite Games and the Historical Context of *Super Mario World*

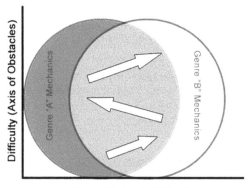

Difficulty (Axis of Obstacles)

Genre "A" Mechanics

Genre "B" Mechanics

Genre (Axis of Abilities)

The y-axis still represents a quantitative measure of difficulty; I call it the *axis of obstacles*. *Donkey Kong* added a new axis, one that represents the qualitative changes of a game moving between two genres. I call this the *axis of abilities*. The back-and-forth movement between genres, unified with Nishikado motion, created a new phenomenon and led to the invention (and eventual dominance) of composite games.

A composite game is one in which a player can use the mechanics and abilities of one genre to solve the problems of another genre, making it a composite of two videogame genres. The first game to exhibit all the features of a modern composite game was *Super Mario Bros.* in 1985, which is both a platformer and an action game. In the case of *Super Mario Bros.*, the player uses platforming game mechanics (jumping) to solve action game problems (defeating enemies). The act of jumping on the head of a Goomba to defeat it typifies the intersection of genres that makes *Super Mario Bros.* so great. The hallmark of composite design is not just a mash-up of genres stretched across the course of a game, but rather the particular way in which the genres are combined. In a composite game, the game's challenges bounce back and forth between the two genres. In *Super Mario Bros.*, this means that the game tends to alternate between platform-intensive levels with lots of open jumps and action-intensive levels that feature more enemies and more combat. The game never stops being both a platformer and an action game, but it tends to alternate its focus between those two genres so that players never get bored of just one kind of activity. This back-and-forth motion between genres leads to a high and sustainable level of engagement that I call *composite flow*. This kind of flow is not the same as traditional psychological flow, but its consciousness-consuming effects are analogous.

In the early days of the composite game (1985 to about 1993), level design was generally defined by powerups that emphasized one genre or another, and *Super Mario World* is a good example of this trend. *Super Mario Bros.* had only one frequently-used powerup that worked as a genre-shifter—the fire-flower—but it's remarkable how often that powerup appears in levels where there are lots of enemies to defeat and not a lot of space to defeat them. In essence, the fire-flower reinforces the level's emphasis on action and combat. This design trend was true for most classic games of the era, in fact. Think of how *Metroid* or *Mega-Man* titles featured powerups that defined the levels in which they appeared, and you can see how designers let powerups guide their design. *Super Mario World* is one of the most essential examples of this kind of level design philosophy in action, as it uses two powerups (the feather and cape) to emphasize one side of the genre composite over another in any given level.

Powerup Declensions and the Evolution of Mario Games

When we talk about a level or section of a level in a composite game that emphasizes one genre more than the other, we're talking about that level's *declension*. (I.e., that level or section declines or "leans" toward one genre, but never abandons either genre.) Typically, the declension of each successive level is different, especially early in a Mario game. If the previous level was a platforming-intensive level, it's likely the current level is going to emphasize action, and vice versa. This is not to say that the Mario team never explored how the level designs themselves could express a genre declension because they frequently did, and we'll see that later in this book.

For the most part, however, Mario games before 1995 shaped their levels around powerups. *Super Mario Bros. 3* is most interesting for the way it uses a huge variety of powerups to achieve the back-and-forth motion of composite flow. Between the fire-flower, raccoon/tanuki tail, wings, Tanuki suit, frog suit, hammer suit, super star, and Kuribo's shoe, the designers were able to push powerup-driven composite design to its logical limit. We can think of *Super Mario Bros. 3* as being the game in which the Mario creators experimented freely with powerups. That experimental attitude resulted in some truly weird and beautiful levels that people still admire today. That weirdness also had some drawbacks in terms of approachability, though. Some levels were much more difficult or more confusing than others.

If *Super Mario Bros. 3* was Mario at his oddest and most experimental, *Super Mario World* is Mario at his most organized and refined. *Super Mario World* has fewer powerups than *Super Mario Bros. 3*, in order to implement a straightforward type of genre-based organization. I visualize that organization in the figure below.

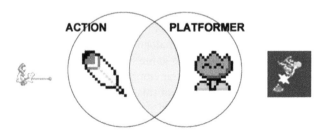

(Note that Yoshi could fit on either side as his tongue attack, dismount-jump, and damage-resistant feet help both action and platformer aspects of the game.) The basic idea is that the fire-flower emphasizes the action elements of the game while the feather emphasizes the platforming aspects. This, admittedly, is a slight simplification. It is possible to use the cape to do action tasks, and the ability to shoot fireballs can make some jumps considerably easier.

 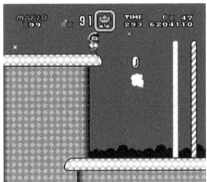

Generally, though, the levels that offer multiple feathers or multiple fire-flowers tend feature a level design that befits the declension that the powerup would suggest.

This doesn't mean that the game features a one-to-one ratio of action to platforming; indeed, there is more platforming than there is action. It also doesn't mean that whole levels must be either in the platforming declension or the action declension. A few levels start off with an action section before switching over to a platforming halfway through, and vice versa. Sometimes, levels will juggle action and platform challenges throughout, and only context in the greater game tells us how to interpret that. By the time the last levels roll around, the player's skills and stamina for challenges are honed to the point that long, varied levels become fun rather than exhausting. Those long levels also allow the designers to synthesize the lessons of various skill themes and to create master-level challenges.

A Brief Recap

This chapter presented a lot of information. Everything explained above will be explained in more detail as we see examples in the game itself. The important ideas to take away from this history, going into Chapters 2 and 3 are these:

1. *Super Mario World* is a composite game. A composite game is a game made up of two or more genres in which the player can use the mechanics of one genre to solve the challenges of another.
2. Like most composite games, *Super Mario World* keeps the player interested by bouncing back and forth between genres. In the case of

Super Mario World, this means that the player alternately encounters platforming and action challenges. Every level has a declension, i.e., it leans toward either platforming or action—but it never stops being both an action game and platformer.

3. *Super Mario World* belongs to the "early period" of composite design, in which designers shaped their levels and skill themes around powerups. *Super Mario World* is the purest example of powerup-based design in the *Mario* series, as it breaks the powerup declensions down into feather/platforming and fire-flower/action.

Measurements and Their Meanings

This chapter will explain how I, along with a colleague, measured *Super Mario World* and what conclusions I drew from those measurements. Everything that can be said about the smallest level of *Super Mario World*'s design comes down to one question: "How difficult is this jump?" Obviously, it's a question that I asked thousands of times. Players don't always consciously ask themselves this question, but it's definitely in the back of their minds, especially on the really tricky jumps. Players have to predict the motion of Mario (or Luigi), the motion of their target, the distance they have to cross, any enemies they need to avoid while in flight, and numerous other factors that affect the difficulty of each individual action. Experienced players can do this in an instant, so it's clear that these elements form a very cohesive whole. The problem for us as designers is figuring out how numerically hard a jump is. Can we unpack the intuitive understanding of this game that so many players have? Can we really break down *Super Mario World* into its constituent parts?

Fortunately, the answer is yes. In fact, *Super Mario World* breaks down quite nicely into its component design elements. From jumps, I was able to deduce challenges, and from challenges, I was able to realize the presence of cadences, and cadences fit together into skill themes. Going back to the beginning, my first task was to figure out ways to meaningfully measure everything in the game. Once everything was measured, things like cadences and skill themes came together quite quickly. This section tries to assemble the same line of thinking and process of discovery that I experienced while researching. The conclusions about these measurements are in Chapter 3, but that chapter and the definitions in it will not make much sense without reading this one first.

Event Height, Event Width, and D-Distance

The first and most important key to understanding the design of *Super Mario World* is the coin-block.

This block is the basic unit of measure in *Super Mario World*—the "atom" of the game. The hardware of the Super Nintendo required that images in the game conform to certain pixel sizes to optimize the file size of assets. Thus, there are no playable surfaces anywhere in the game that are not made up of an integer block length. There are no heights that are not made up of a whole number of blocks. Some moving platforms pass through heights that are not evenly divisible by blocks, but even these come to rest at block-level. Some objects appear to sit in spaces not evenly divisible by a coin-block, too, but their "hit box" is almost always at an effective integer mark. Therefore, every jump event in the game, even underwater events, can be measured precisely.

Mario's ability to jump to any given height is dependent upon the amount of momentum he has. With no momentum, Mario can jump on top of a platform four blocks above the position of his feet. With one block of lateral momentum he can jump to a platform five blocks above the level of his feet. With eleven blocks of momentum, he can jump as high as the top of the sixth block above his feet.

If he has the cape, 11 blocks of momentum will enable Mario to soar high enough that measuring that height is pointless. You'll notice, of course, that these momentum levels correspond to block-lengths. The 11-block momentum benchmark is important because it frequently prevents Mario from using the soaring cape ability to bypass levels (or sections of levels) that lack platforms of sufficient length. The designers of *Super Mario World* made level design easier on themselves by doing this; as long as they restricted platforms to lengths of less than 10, they could exert some control on how the player would approach a level.

There's also the issue of how far Mario has to go *laterally* when jumping. Most jumps involve a lateral distance, which also breaks down nicely into block-lengths. At no momentum, Mario can jump from block one to block six, a distance of five blocks.

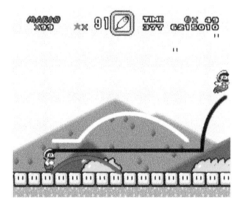

At any level of momentum before a full run, he can jump from block one to block nine (distance of eight), and at a full run he can cover 12 blocks. All of this, of course, assumes a flat area; any vertical distance involved in the jump will change the figures significantly. None of this takes into account the use of the cape powerup. The cape extends the fall time on a typical jump to about three times its normal length. It doesn't significantly affect the speed of the lateral motion (what we'll call the x vector), but by allowing the jump's vertical motion (y vector) to last longer, jumps can go farther before Mario hits the ground again. Of course, the player can use the cape while at a full run to go so far across the level that measuring is pointless; only a wall, ceiling, or enemy will stop him.

There are three important statistics that come out of these measurements: delta height, delta width, and d-distance. (Delta means the change between two or more points of data.) The most obvious place to start measuring jumps is the *danger distance*, or *d-distance* for short. This statistic is probably the most important one in this book. The d-distance is the amount of lateral distance that

Mario has to cover in a single jump event. In the screens below, you can see how I measure this.

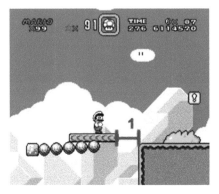 

You'll notice I don't measure diagonally. Because of the way that vectors, intercepts, and powerups in *Super Mario World* work, diagonals aren't any more meaningful than the mere lateral distance unless there's another element like an intercept present, and then it's the intercept that's really meaningful. D-distance measures the size of deadly obstacles Mario is trying to avoid, whether it's a bottomless pit or some kind of damage floor.

The next most obvious point of study is changes in height during a jump event (delta height). In the jump pictured here, Mario is ascending. A number alone doesn't explain if the jump is difficult, however, so let's break it down further. This jump goes up; jumps that go up are more challenging than jumps that go down. The reason for this is that Mario loses his momentum when he's going up (unless he's flying with the cape or Blue Yoshi), but when going down his momentum tends to stay the same and can be easily controlled with a cape-glide. Anyone who has played the game will instantly know that the right hand jump pictured below is easier—even with a larger d-distance—because it is descending. When Mario begins a descending event, he usually has a lot more time to get into the right x-position. The y-position will take care of itself because of the pull of in-game gravity. Mario is already falling the whole time, so the player doesn't really have to worry about that—especially if he has the cape, which will greatly extend the fall and give the player a ton of time to guide Mario downwards. There are exceptions to the rule, but it's almost always harder to jump upwards than downwards.

The trickiest measurement we have to make is the width metric. First, we should define what we mean by width. The starting width of a jump event is the amount of horizontal space that the player has available to begin a jump event. Starting platform width matters mostly because it determines how much momentum Mario can accumulate before jumping. Starting width is pretty easy to measure, but landing width is often complicated by factors other than the size of the platform.

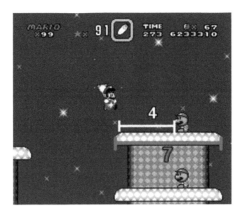

There's an enemy approaching that will damage Mario if the player doesn't avoid it. Can the player simply drop Mario onto the head of the oncoming Koopa? Maybe, but the problem is that when this jump begins, the Koopa is offscreen, and so by the time the player sees it, Mario might not have enough height to bounce of its head. Therefore, the real target/landing width of this jump is four blocks because that's the width available for landing between the edge and the enemy. Most of the time, the starting and target widths are not so complicated, but it is an issue that the player has to confront from time to time.

Just as it is more difficult to perform a jump that ends higher than it began, it is more difficult to perform a jump that ends on a platform smaller than the one Mario jumps off. The width-specific difficulty of a jump is usually determined by the size of the landing platform. It's not especially hard to start a jump on any platform wider than one block, but it's definitely harder to land on a narrow target because of Mario's momentum. The general idea is that the wider the target is, the easier the jump will be. That said, the hardest jumps are the ones that both begin *and* end on very small platforms. We'll get to talking about that momentum in just a moment, but what I found overall is that across the course of a level, the starting platform for a jump event doesn't need to change to make that jump harder. It's the landing platform's width that reveals if there are any really meaningful changes in the sizes of things. That said, starting platform width matters in a few levels that require lots of momentum and don't provide space for it, like Outrageous or Forest of Illusion 4.

There is one last point of concern for the measurement of space, and that is the use of soft sizes. An object with a "soft" size is any object for which the disparity between the graphics and collision box favors the player. That's a little wordy, so let's use an example. The big bullet pictured below is an obvious case: although the animated object is quite large, the part of it that can hurt Mario is smaller than it seems like it ought to be.

When it comes to platforms, however, the sizes are almost always *larger* than they appear to be, as you can see above. The size of the object is almost always more favorable to the player than it looks like it ought to be. Shigeru Miyamoto was a pioneer of this technique, going back as far as the barrels in *Donkey Kong*. Play a few other arcade games that don't employ soft sizes, and you will quickly see what a difference they can make to a player's feelings of euphoria or frustration.

Intercepts

An intercept is an enemy timed and placed so that it interferes with a jump that Mario needs to make. The prototypical intercept is a Wing-Koopa that patrols a vertical path above a bottomless pit. If Mario jumps at the wrong time, the Koopa will intercept him along his path, sending him to his death. The general rule for intercepts is that the more of them there are, the harder the jump and/or challenge will be.

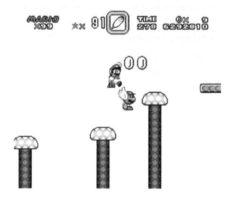

This rule of quantity is only true up to a point. Eventually the screen can become so saturated with Wing Koopas that Mario can't help but land on one after another, earning him points and possible extra lives, but this is rare. It's also true that different kinds and speeds of intercept are more difficult than intercepts that are uniform in quality. The last important thing to know is what intercepts are not. This enemy is *not* an intercept:

This enemy is causing Mario to jump. This enemy begins the jump event, and therefore cannot also be an intercept that alters the jump event. The Wing Koopa in the first example is not the cause of the jump event, but rather an obstacle that modifies the jump event. The gap between the platforms is the cause of that jump; the Wing Koopa merely makes it harder.

Penalty

It is also important to measure the results of failure, which I call "penalty." Penalty specifically refers to the result of a failed jump event. That is, if Mario needs to jump from platform A to platform B and fails, the penalty is the result of that failure. Only guaranteed penalties are measured for this book. That is to say, if there are enemies in a pit below, there's a chance Mario could land in that pit without taking damage. This is merely a *risk* that the player must deal with, rather than a guaranteed result. The most iconic penalty comes from the bottomless pit, which will definitely cause the loss of a life. Not all jumps penalize the player with death, however. Some jumps merely do damage and some have no penalty except having to do the jump over.

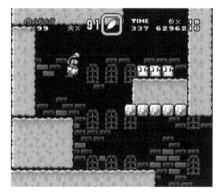
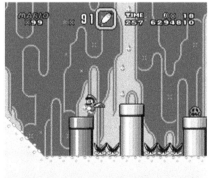

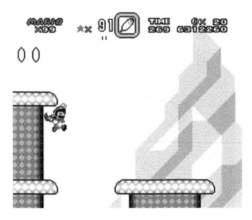

I rate these penalties with numbers for the sake of consistency and comparability. If the penalty for failing a jump is only having to try that jump again, and Mario doesn't lose a life or take any damage, the penalty rating is a zero. Jumps in which the penalty is damage but not necessarily death are rated one. Instant death pits are rated two. Throughout this book, we'll see how penalty, but especially *changes* in penalty, are a meaningful part of level design. Deviations from that standard penalty are what tell us, as players, that the designer is pressuring us to learn and perform in new ways.

Vectors

Although vectors only need to be measured once, they're nevertheless very important to the game—and they're also important because in *Super Mario World* they've changed significantly from earlier Mario titles. For our purposes, we can define vectors as the forces of momentum a moving object has in the world of *Super Mario World*. Real world vectors are significantly different from *Super Mario World* vectors, so disregard your knowledge of physics because it will not help you understand this game. Mario's vectors in *Super Mario World* have two properties: magnitude and direction. Acceleration and deceleration are totally unrealistic from a real-world point of view, but they make complete sense from the point of view of game design. As we saw above, Mario doesn't gain running speed in a linear, asymptotic, or gradual fashion. Rather, Mario has three speeds and he switches from one to the next after passing a certain number of uninterrupted blocks of distance. This is our x-vector, the side-to-side motion of Mario in the game. As for the other direction, it's important to note that Mario's jump speed is completely static. His jumps simply rise and fall without perceptible acceleration or deceleration physics. He jumps at one speed and falls at almost exactly the same speed. (Falling takes just a few frames longer than jumping, to give the player a little more time to land, but it is imperceptible to most people.) There is also a very slight pause (about three frames long) in between ascent and descent. The only things that can modify his jump velocity are the presence of water, a springboard, or the use of the cape powerup in a glide.

The x-vector and y-vector are of enormous importance to the design of the game because one of them always has a fixed magnitude. In most levels, the y-vector has a static magnitude; just as noted above, Mario's upward jump motion only has two speeds. Even when soaring upwards with the cape or falling from a great height, Mario only ever moves along the y-axis at either jump speed or at cape-glide speed—that's all. Even soaring up onto the highest platforms is a manipulation of the x-vector; Mario can only gain that extra height by increasing his x-vector magnitude (run speed) to its maximum. This is the reason why platform width is such an important datum: Mario needs that width to gain height. Once Mario is in the air, however, there are only two speeds at which he can move up and down: fall speed or cape speed. (Some master-level players can "blink" the cape glide in certain situations involving longer falls to fake a third fall speed, but this is very hard to do. There is a built-in cooldown on button presses that will start a glide, and so most players cannot switch back and forth between falling and gliding with meaningful results.) This means that in most levels, much of the problem-solving work done by the player consists of these skills:

1. Getting Mario to the right momentum
2. Standing at/jumping from the right place
3. Jumping at the right time
4. Avoiding the sudden appearance of enemies

Those four skills correspond to the skill themes in the game, respectively: the preservation of momentum theme, the periodic enemies theme, the moving targets theme, and the intercepts theme. We'll cover those in more detail Chapter 3.

Of course, there are also the water levels, and as you might expect these levels place a much greater emphasis on solving problems via the y-axis, but this doesn't mean the necessary skills have changed. What's really happened is that the game has literally turned sideways. In a water level, the vector scheme is reversed; now the x-vector magnitude (speed) is static and the y-vector speed can actually change. In a water level, the player has control over Mario's ascent and descent speeds, and can zoom along the y-axis quite quickly and with a great amount of control. The player is unable, however, to change Mario's x-axis swim speed in a meaningful way. There are only two speeds that Mario can move laterally in these levels: walk or swim. (Skilled players can cancel Mario's swim animation for a slight boost in speed, but only when directly underneath a platform. This is not often possible.)

Many of the challenges in a water level have to do with quickly going up or down in the water to avoid enemies or other obstacles. You can see how enemies in water levels are staggered so that Mario can ascend or descend between them.

Shooting these gaps in a dry level would require some serious jumping skills, but in a water level, it's not hard. In water levels, it's not that the designers have removed the platforms, but that *everything* has become a platform. Mario can jump at any time; all empty space is a platform. Naturally, this strips away the possibility of the designers using the platforming-declension themes (all water levels are either intercepts, periodic enemies or outside of the themes altogether). The moving targets and preservation of momentum themes are built upon the fact that Mario has to commit to a jump in the right way. The water allows Mario to "jump" (in a loose sense) at any time. The only problem with these challenges is that with fewer inherent design possibilities, the levels can become a bit repetitive. Each water level is different from the others, but they can feel slow and similar throughout because the designers have fewer options.

Historical Changes in Vectors

Despite all the detail laid out about vectors, the momentum mechanics present in *Super Mario World* are actually a simplification from earlier titles in the series. In *Super Mario Bros* and *Super Mario Bros. 3*, when Mario was moving at full speed, he was unable to come to a complete and sudden stop on an open plane. Instead, he would "slide" about half a block in the direction his momentum had been carrying him. This made for some frequent problems when landing on a narrow platform, since Mario's momentum could easily carry him straight over the edge into pits and enemies. To compensate for this, many players would do a momentum-breaking backwards-jump in order to land on a platform.

As if the momentum weren't enough, there was a very short (but potentially deadly) input lag/cooldown on Mario's ability to jump. These mechanics were eliminated in *Super Mario World*. The player's ability to stop Mario's horizontal momentum is now about as close to perfectly precise as human and technological limitations would allow at the time.

The second major change in game-physics is in the arc of Mario's jump. In *Super Mario Bros.* and *Super Mario Bros. 3*, Mario's jump arc was clearly divisible into sections. It's easiest to understand if you see the diagram below.

The first part of Mario's jump is a rapid ascent; the second part slows down before beginning the descent of the arc. The descent starts off slowly, and then returns to the initial speed of the jump. The reasoning behind this two-speed arc is that by giving Mario more time at the peak of his jump, it's easier to land on a target like the head of a Koopa. (There may also be technological reasons for this, but we can only account for the design effects here.) The problem is that a two-speed jump makes the hardest jumps harder. Jumps that feature things like intercepts or moving targets are complicated by the fact that a player doesn't just have to predict Mario's landing point, but also how the slower, second stage of his arc might collide with the obstacles along the way. Eventually the player will learn how to handle those physics, but wouldn't it be more straightforward just to have a uniform jump motion everywhere? *Super Mario World* changes things so that the motion of Mario's jump is almost uniform throughout. In *Super Mario World*, when Mario jumps, he ascends almost exactly at the same speed he descends (the descent is imperceptibly longer), with only a tiny pause (about 3-4 frames) at the apex of the jump.

The meaning we find in a study of the vectors in *Super Mario World* is less obvious than d-distance or delta-height or any of those measurements. The refined and intuitive vector system in this game is in place to make this game not just accessible to a broad audience, but also to shift the primary focus of the player from systems mastery (physics) to content mastery (learning patterns in level design). While players who grew up on the earlier games might complain that this makes the jump mechanics too easy, the decision ultimately allows the designers to come up with more elaborate and inventive challenges in the architecture of the levels themselves. It's much more rewarding for the player to fail a jump because they're hit by a fireball they're aware of than it is for them to simply slip off a cliff edge they weren't even paying attention to.

3

Challenges, Cadences, and Skill Themes

The purpose of a *Reverse Design* isn't merely to accumulate data, especially since there is a ton of data on videogames these days. The greater purpose of a *Reverse Design* is to figure out what those data mean so that readers can learn from the masters. Thus, the second step in the writing in this book was to look for patterns in the data. One of them is obvious: across the course of the game, the various jumps get harder. Donut Plains 3 and Chocolate Island 3 are almost the same level, except that the latter level has a larger average d-distance, significantly more enemies, and far fewer safe platforms.

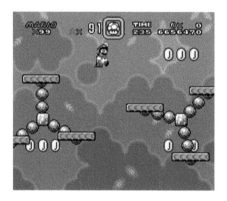 

This is something everyone knows: the game gets harder. One thing that surprised me, however, is that most levels *did not* get harder this way. There was no consistent quantitative measure that showed why later levels would be more difficult than earlier levels. Generally, the data suggest that every numerical factor in the game (distance between jumps, number of enemies, size of platforms) either peaks or plateaus before the halfway point of the game.

Interestingly, though, there is very consistent evidence that individual levels become more complex toward their respective ends, and so this is where most of the research was done. In almost any level in the game, the relation between the end of the level and the beginning is fairly obvious.

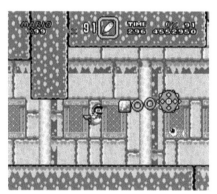 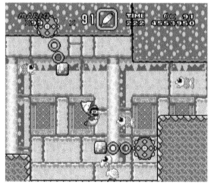

For example, these are the first and last encounters possible with the Ball'n'Chain enemy in Vanilla Fortress. It's pretty obvious that the second instance is a lot more difficult than the first, for both quantitative (amount of safe space, number of intercepts) and qualitative (variety of dangerous objects) reasons. This is true of almost every level in the game. Therefore, it stands to reason that the structure of levels might have something to tell us about how the game gets harder.

Challenges

To understand how levels grow more complex, we have to break them down into their constituent parts. A challenge is the essential unit of content in a level. It is a cluster of actions that must be undertaken in one attempt, with periods of relative safety on either side of it. The safe spaces between challenges are the best way to figure out when a challenge begins and ends. For example, the first and third shots here are the beginning and end of this challenge from Yoshi's Island 3.

The challenge begins and ends in safety. Most challenges are like this; it seems that the design team wanted players to be able to plan ahead a little bit when going through any challenge.

Cadences

A cadence is the progression of challenges explained by their relation to the standard challenge. Almost everything in a level relates back to the standard challenge clearly. The only way to fully understand challenges is by seeing how they interact, so we'll begin by defining that interaction.

Standard Challenge

The standard challenge is the first and most basic form of the challenges that are developed in the course of a level. Sometimes the first challenge in a level isn't the standard, but this is rare, and I have made a note in levels where this is the case. Nevertheless, a standard challenge is usually simple, and no subsequent challenge in the cadence will be simpler, qualitatively. My favorite level for illustrating cadences is Soda Lake. This is the standard challenge for Soda Lake:

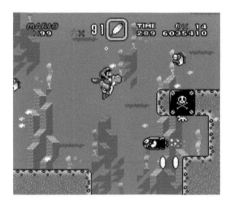

The standard challenge contains a torpedo launcher with some accompanying Blurps. We'll see how this grows in complexity as the level progresses.

Expansion Challenge

An expansion takes an existing challenge and increases some part of it quantitatively. An expansion challenge doesn't change from the standard challenge qualitatively (or at least not by much). In Soda Lake, this is the first expansion:

The number of launchers goes up, but there's still the same amount of swimming space and the level architecture hasn't increased in complexity. Although the position of the launchers has changed, it hasn't evolved—it's still on the edge of the screen rather than bisecting it or covering all of it in launchers.

There are many other ways to create an expansion challenge. These variables are common, too:

> *D-Distance*: The classic expansion in Mario is to simply increase the width of the pits he has to jump over. This makes jumping more difficult in an obvious way. Most of the time, increases in d-distance will accompany other changes, too.

> *Delta Height*: As we saw earlier, the bigger the difference in height, the harder it is to complete a jump, especially when jumping upwards. Often in an expansion challenge, an easy height will become a hard one as it expands, but everything else will remain the same.

> *Intercepts*: The number of intercepts in a challenge can go up, which makes the jump more difficult, up to a point. Typically, an expansion in intercepts means that a greater quantity of the same monster appears in a new challenge.

> *Penalty*: Finally, the penalty of a challenge can be expanded. This usually means that the standard challenge has a penalty of one (damage) and the expansion raises the penalty to two (instant death). The reason for this is that the game is using the expansion as a spot-check. A spot-check is a challenge that forces the player to demonstrate that they can execute a certain skill (or combination thereof) before progressing any farther. There's usually no way to fumble through a spot-check. Sometimes Mario might take some damage, and then run through a challenge while he's temporarily immune, but in a spot-check this is impossible because of the raised penalty. The good thing about expansion challenges is that even when they expand to spot-checks, the challenge is always something which the player has already done.

Evolution Challenge

In contrast to an expansion, an evolution is a qualitative change that uses all the same skills as some previous challenge but in a more qualitatively complex situation. In Soda Lake, the first evolution is this one.

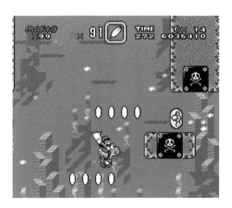

Here, the two launchers from the previous expansion are split up to cover more of the screen. The quantitative elements are mostly the same: there are still two launchers. The configuration of the launchers makes for an undeniably more complex challenge, however. Now, rather than having one clear path to take, the player has to assess the two possible paths and choose the more likely. This is one form of the greater complexity that an evolution challenge accomplishes.

Note that evolutions and expansions don't only evolve or expand from the standard challenge. The challenge above is actually an evolution upon the expansion, which in turn was an expansion upon the standard challenge. To notate it three different ways:

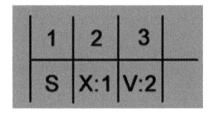

1. The Standard Challenge
2. Then an *expansion* (X) upon the standard
3. Then an *evolution* (V) upon that expansion

For a more in-depth look at notating the cadences of levels in *Super Mario World* and a statistical analysis on them, see Chapter 10, which contains lots of extra info about them, including maps and charts.

Mutation: A mutation challenge is an iteration of any challenge that neither increases the complexity by evolution nor expands the quantitative aspects of the challenge that is being mutated. Rather, a mutation challenge simply reiterates a challenge in a slightly different way that is more or less equally challenging as its parent challenge. To go back to Vanilla Fortress (because Soda Lake has no mutations), these challenges are mutations of one another.

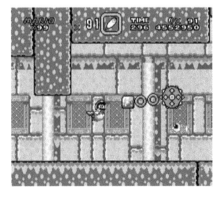
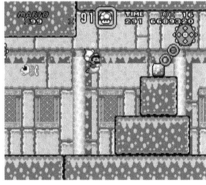

Although the second challenge has less theoretical space, it doesn't have less functional space. That is to say, Mario doesn't need a path both above and below the mace as it swings in loops: he can only take one path anyway. Thus, the path is effectively the same size in both. In the second case, he merely needs to swim up and shoot the gap with the slightest amount of forethought for timing. The level is just giving the player a different look and asking him/her to fully explore the physics and pace of going up and down in the water. It's not more complex, it's just different.

Mutation challenges are important because not every single challenge can get more difficult or complex, or else many levels would become tiresome. Part of establishing a good sense of pacing in level design lies in knowing when to give the player a break or an easy challenge to restore their morale and give their concentration a rest.

Training Wheels Challenge

A training-wheels challenge is designed to allow players to use new skills in a low-risk, easy-to-understand environment. Training-wheels challenges are especially prevalent in early levels because they tend to occur in places where the player is using entirely new skills or new combinations of skills. To make acquisition of these skills easy and not frustrating, the designers do two things:

1. Break what would be a standard challenge in any other level into its smallest component parts, teaching players how to execute each individual part of the challenge before putting them together (whereas an evolution would add something new).
2. Use one or more methods to reduce the penalty of the challenge down to zero.

You can see how this is a training-wheels challenge because although the player can fail, the penalty of that failure is removed.

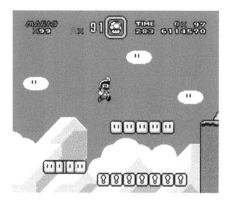

Plenty of challenges start off in simple forms and then assume more complex forms later in the level, but these are usually cases of evolution or expansion challenges, discussed above. A training-wheels challenge breaks everything down to its smallest parts, separating them down into single-element segments. Additionally, the penalty must come down. That is to say, if the standard challenge in the theoretical "normal" level features a bottomless pit, the training-wheels challenge either puts a floor over that pit, or some other means of reducing the penalty to zero. The point of the training-wheels challenge is to introduce the player to using new skills in the same way training-wheels work on a bike.

Punctuating Challenge

The punctuating challenge is a kind of punctuation mark in the sentence of a cadence. These are used as breaks in levels during which the level does not get more complex. A punctuating challenge is not related the standard challenge in any clear way. It is not an evolution or expansion of the main design ideas in the level. It is simply a break from the progress of the cadence that meets the definition of a challenge. I tend not to mention these because they're not related to the cadence. There are a few noteworthy examples in the level analysis section. The important thing to know is that if you are analyzing a level and find one of these, you are not making a mistake. Not everything in the level is related to the main cadence.

Crossover Challenge

A crossover challenge is a challenge that features a brief shift from one declension to another. These are generally brief and only occur in longer levels. In *Super Mario World*, the crossover challenges are usually built out of the complementary theme. That is, if the level is built around the preservation of momentum theme, the crossover challenge is built out of the enemy intercepts theme, and vice versa. Sometimes, especially later in the game, the crossover challenges are not made up of the complementary theme, but predominantly they are. Crossover challenges are important to a cadence because they arise out of the complement theme and tend to work with the skills already in play in the cadence, rather than merely punctuating them.

Expansion by Contraction

This is just an expansion challenge that operates by narrowing the amount of safe space in a challenge. Like all oxymoronic terms, it exists because it describes a phenomenon more concisely and precisely than anything else would. Most expansions are literal expansions of some numerical element; but in these challenges, they're reductions in the size of safe space in a jump or the size of the platforms involved.

Reward by Fun

Occasionally, the designers will throw in a section in the game that is significantly easier than what surrounds it. The primary criterion for a reward by fun is the availability of non-death failure. Usually, this means that Mario has to do something unusual (relative to the surrounding challenges) to get a reward. He can lose that reward, but it's almost impossible for him to come to real harm; the only penalty is not succeeding. The Switch Palaces are good examples of this.

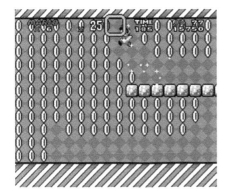 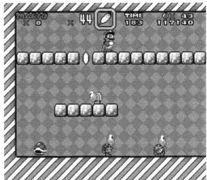

There is a challenge in each palace that the player can mess up and not get all the potential rewards, but Mario's death is pretty unlikely. This kind of challenge exists throughout the game, often as a kind of "comic relief" in the middle of otherwise difficult levels.

Skill Themes, The Top Level of the Design

Just as challenges add up into cadences, levels add up into skill themes. A skill theme is a series of levels that develop a consistent set of player skills through the use of fundamentally similar but ever-evolving challenges. While the entire game of *Super Mario World* gets harder, the exact methods are not necessarily quantifiable, or at least not consistently demonstrable as a set of quantitative increases. The qualitative evolution across the course of a game is clear when looking at skill themes, however. By isolating levels that share common architecture and skill requirements, we can compare them apples-to-apples, as it were. How do we identify which levels are in the same theme? This is where the knowledge of game design history becomes particularly important. Skill themes in a composite game are the material embodiment of composite design. A designer can take advantage of the various elements of the contributing composites to get specific effects in any given level. This is a little hard to understand out of context, but *Super Mario World* gives us many good examples. There are four major skill themes in the game, and they lay out well on a matrix.

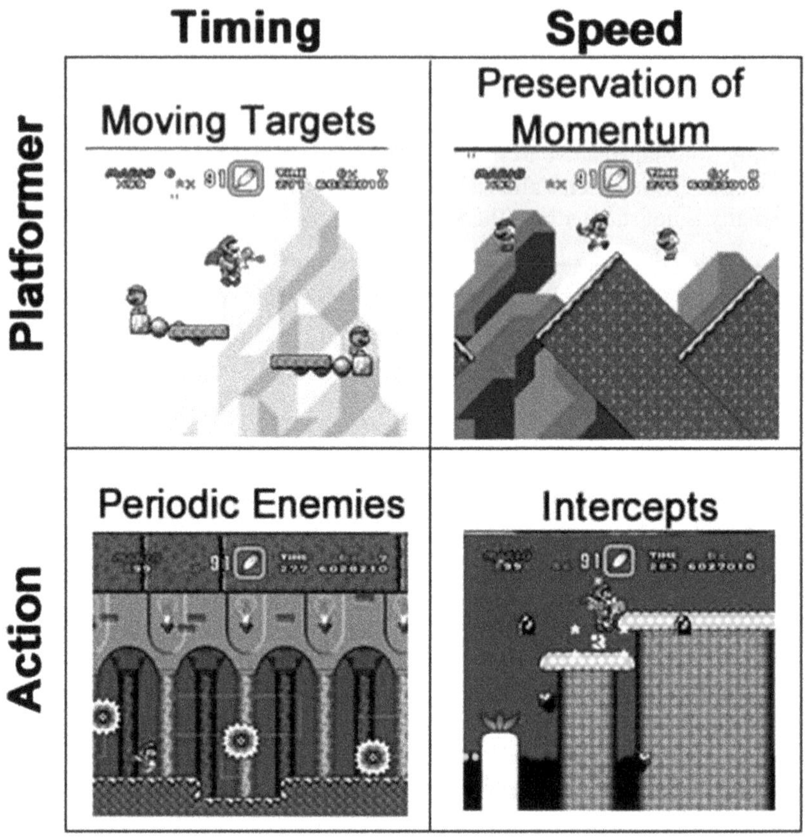

Timing / **Speed**

Platformer

Moving Targets / Preservation of Momentum

Action

Periodic Enemies / Intercepts

Naturally, two of the categories that are being crossed here are the two genres that *Super Mario World* combines: action and platforming. The other two categories are not historically derived, but are still plain to see in the game. "Speed" simply means that the level in question forces the player to steer Mario through challenges at a relatively high speed. Sometimes this is an obvious obstacle, like a sinking platform that requires Mario's to jump off before it drops away. Sometimes it's an oncoming wave of enemies that would be much harder to defeat than to avoid, and this requires a quick reaction. In both cases, sustained speed and reflexes are more useful than slow, deliberately-timed jumps.

On the other hand, there are many cases in which jumping headlong into a challenge at full momentum is either impossible or inadvisable. These are the timing-sensitive situations pictured in the graphic. It might be possible for a skilled player to make the jump to the next platform with full momentum, but it's probably a lot easier to just wait a second or two for the platform to come back along its route. Similarly, a master level player might be able to react precisely enough to shoot tiny gaps in groups of enemies, but it's probably easier to wait for them to be in a better position. Recognizing these thematic cues in the environment is a key meta-skill that the player learns pretty quickly—mostly by dying a few times. Just because the player recognizes that a section is action-oriented or momentum-oriented doesn't mean that they've solved the section. A skill theme is, after all, made up of a variety of skills that the player has to master.

The definitions of everything written above are not meant to exist as concepts in isolation. The next section, which contains an analysis of every level in the game (except Bowser's Castle), will illustrate all of these concepts copiously. Additionally, it should be noted here that not every level is in a skill theme. There are 13 levels that are outside of the skill themes, and two levels (Vanilla Secret 1, Gnarly) that occupy a mini-theme of their own. That's less than a quarter of all levels, however, and so the skill themes do account for most of the game's organization.

4

The Moving Targets Skill Theme

Introduction to Level Analysis

As the introduction noted, the quantitative aspects of the game like the distance of jumps, the number of intercepts, and the HP of enemies do not consistently increase across the course of the game. By the third section of the game (Vanilla Dome), the growth of the numerical aspects of the game hits a plateau. For example, the level with the most intercepts is Vanilla Secret 2, right in the middle of the game. The level with the highest average d-distance is in the second castle level, well before the halfway point. With a few insignificant exceptions (the level with the smallest average platform size is Valley of Bowser 3, for example), most of the expanding dimensions of the game peak long before the end. Therefore, our goal is to figure out how the skill themes develop qualitative complexity from beginning to end.

There are two ways in which this qualitative increase in difficulty happens: *iteration and accumulation*. Iteration is the process by which a theme introduces various mechanical iterations upon the same skill. In essence, iteration is about exploring all the possibilities for a single game design theme. Usually, the later iterations are more complex and difficult than the earlier ones, but it's not always so, and the difference isn't drastic. For example, the moving targets theme begins with a platform that only moves when Mario stands on it. It ends with a platform that doesn't even carry Mario with it when it moves. Somewhere in the middle, it picks up an irregular path, but none of the individual challenges in this gradual evolution are that much harder than their immediate ancestor.

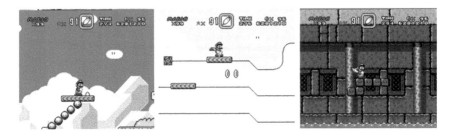

When the later stages of the game begin, the designers move out of iteration and into accumulation, in which all of the ideas introduced during iteration are stacked on top of each other (figuratively) in the same few levels. For example, the intercepts theme has introduced several different kinds of intercepts with different kinds of behavior. This challenge in Outrageous contains almost all of them at once!

All the themes in the game eventually proceed from iteration to accumulation, although each one does so in a different way and at a different speed. Included as the headnote to each theme is a summary of how that theme develops through iteration and accumulation, which also serves as a useful introduction to the theme.

Note that this document analyzes every level in the game except Bowser's Castle and does not examine any of the castle boss fights. Bowser's Castle is merely a pastiche of level design ideas better examined in other levels. I also did not examine the boss fights. Most of the game design in *Super Mario World* is still relevant to modern games; the bosses are not. The bosses have aged badly. This seems to be a problem many Mario games face—that the boss fights are of a much poorer quality than the rest of the game. It does not diminish the quality of the game as a whole, however.

The moving targets theme is probably the simplest theme from the perspective of the player, and yet it is probably the most complex from the perspective of the designer. From the player's perspective, this theme is relatively simple because it's all about one skill: the timing jump. Because the platforms in this theme are usually moving, there's almost always a "best" time to jump, if the player can identify it. Because of this dynamic, the measurements of jumps in this theme were all based on these optimal moments. Assuming the player makes optimal jumps, this theme features the lowest average d-distance, the second-lowest average delta height, and the lowest average number of intercepts. The theme also features the smallest average platform width of any theme, which, combined with the previous traits, suggests that this theme isn't about momentum or reactions. This theme is all about one skill, and that skill is jumping at the right time. The kinds of platforms the player encounters evolve consistently across the course of the theme, but that transition is so smooth and focused that the player will probably view this theme as being the easiest and most straightforward.

From the designer's perspective, the moving targets theme is probably the most complex theme. The reason for this is that the theme does more with iteration and less with accumulation than any other theme. It's relatively easy for the designers to pile design ideas on top of one another. Building the levels Outrageous (intercepts theme) or Valley Fortress (periodic enemies theme) was probably a relatively easy task. All the designers had to do was use enemies and obstacles already seen in other levels, and then playtest the results. (Playtesting is at least 75% of the process of making any game, re-using existing game mechanics cuts down on that process.) Yet those are two of the most challenging levels in the game from the perspective of the player.

The moving targets theme rarely re-uses content and hardly ever re-uses content in a cumulative way. This may not have been out of a planned avoidance of accumulation, but instead because of a practical problem. Donut Plains 2 illustrates this well, as it features rotating platforms, looping tracked platforms, and linear tracked platforms in sequence, but none of those platforms is ever truly "stacked" on top of another. How could they be combined? In an accumulation, the player has to deal with multiple game design ideas from a theme at the same time. If there were looping platforms and rotating platforms and linear platforms all in one challenge, it would simply be a case of the player choosing one and ignoring the others, and that's not accumulation. Although the invention of skill themes was probably serendipity, I do believe the designers consciously pursued a strategy of iteration followed by accumulation. Because accumulation is difficult to execute this theme, there's more iteration to flush out the amount of content the designers needed in the game.

Iteration is more difficult than accumulation in most cases because it requires the designer to not just innovate, but to *invent* mechanics. Invention within the constraints of a single idea (a moving platform) is difficult because it requires a constant stream of new ideas, and because each of those ideas has to be implemented (and bug-tested) in a level for the first time. Thus, this theme was probably the hardest for the designers. The *Super Mario World* team did a remarkable job with it, however. Take a look:

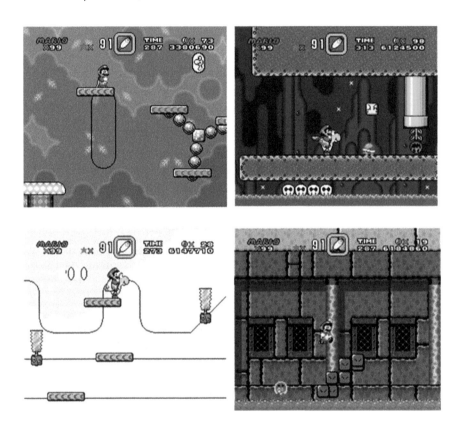

The designers work their way through a lot of iteration here. The theme starts with simple rotating and contracting platforms in Yoshi's Island 3, the absolute simplest forms of the idea in this game. (This game is curiously devoid of platforms that move up and down in straight lines.) The rotating platforms evolve in Donut Plains 2, and then evolve again mid-level into the looping tracked platform, and finally the linear tracked platform. Cheese Bridge develops the linear tracked platform across a whole level, even turning it on its side with the moving rope. Forest Secret Area builds a level out of two moving platforms and not much else--and results in a beautiful illustration of the action/platform composite. Roy's Castle introduces the final iteration in the theme with the caterpillar platform that moves out from under Mario, not carrying him with it. Even the last moving targets level, Way Cool, is only a series of expansions and evolutions upon ideas already developed in Cheese Bridge—no real accumulation takes place.

The only level in which we see a concrete accumulation of previous design ideas is Larry's Castle, and even then, it's slight. In this section, the player is separated from a caterpillar platform. This combines ideas seen in Vanilla Dome 3 and Roy's Castle.

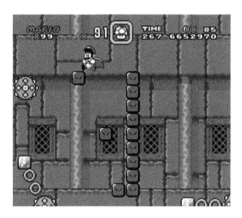

The first part of this challenge is the most elegant, I think, in that it not only brings back separation from the platform but does so in a more advanced way. Instead of merely having to keep up with the platform through some periodic enemy obstacles, the player actually has to do some platforming with it. Moreover, although speed is of the essence here, this isn't like a typical preservation-of-momentum challenge. This is simply a matter of knowing how fast Mario has to go in order to keep up and making two tricky but not overwhelming jumps to do so. After this, the rest of the separation is fairly standard, although the inclusion of proper periodic enemies is a definite evolution over the Piranha Plants of Vanilla Dome 3.

Overall, there's a lot for a designer to learn from this theme about how to make the most out of a single idea. Many of the ideas from this theme have clear descendants in Yoshi's Island and even contemporary 2D Mario games. The moving target is one of the oldest and most-used ideas in 2D platforming, and having a big "vocabulary," as it were, of moving platforms continues to be a useful resource.

Yoshi's Island 3

Super Mario World introduces the moving targets theme by constructing a level with lots of training-wheels challenges and not that much cadence development. Assuming that the player has already completed the Yellow Switch Palace (which is likely), most of the jumps in Yoshi's Island 3 have a penalty of zero because of the yellow !-block floors below. This safety net is especially generous considering that there are hardly any d-distances larger than two, and almost none of those involve a positive change in height.

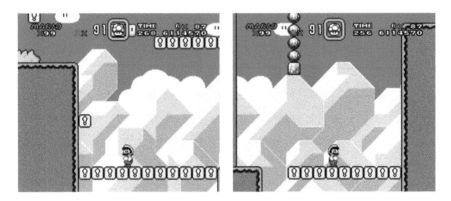

As was mentioned above, one of the clear indications of a training-wheels challenge is a reduction in penalty, and those yellow blocks certainly accomplish that.

This level also shows us the other aspect of the training-wheels challenge, in which a normal challenge is broken down into its component parts. The swinging platforms pictured below are a good example of this. Whereas most moving platforms are going to be moving all the time, these start in a stationary position; it's only when Mario lands on them that they start moving.

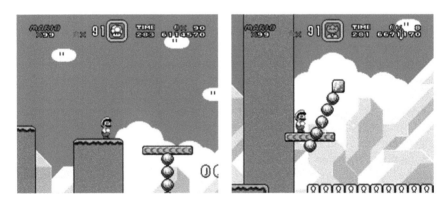

The only part of these first few challenges that involves motion is the "dismount." As Part II of this document explains, the difficulty of a jump is determined more by the landing area rather than by the starting area. In this case, the starting area is a small moving platform (width of three), but the landing area is a wide, empty, stationary cliff-top. Essentially, the game is able to introduce the moving targets theme while taking away the hardest part of it: jumping onto a moving target. Factor in the safety net of yellow blocks below, and it's clear how much the designers wanted to go easy on the player.

The skill that the designers are trying to teach, in this case, is how to perform a timing jump. That is, the player needs to be able to look at various moving targets and intuit the best time to jump during the target's rotation. This will often mean that the player has to be patient and focus on the targets rather than thinking about Mario's momentum. The timing jump is the foundation of the moving targets skill theme. Although it is a simple skill to learn, the designers have to drill it into the player because the context for the jump will become increasingly complex as the game progresses.

Inasmuch as the level does anything resembling a cadence, it's in the way that the training-wheels slowly fall off in the manner of an expansion challenge.

This isn't a typical expansion challenge, but it is true to the spirit of the type—there is a gradual quantitative increase in the difficulty of the challenges. It's just unusual in that the quantitative change is in the training-wheels—the penalty increases to two. That's the only real progression in the level. Challenges like these aren't really increases in complexity, just different versions the same thing.

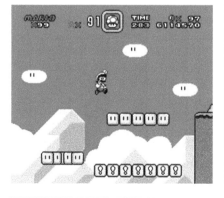

These could be called mutations, although they are serving more of an educational "you can do it" purpose than they will later in the game.

Donut Plains 3

Before we dive into the individual details of DP3, it's worth mentioning that this level, just like Yoshi's Island 3, focuses on the skill of waiting. Even the most novice players know how to wait. This is an elegant way of acclimating new players to a tricky skill.

Donut Plains 3 introduces most of the types of moving platforms and pertinent challenges that will appear for the rest of the game—although most of the challenges appear in fairly easy forms to start. The first change from Yoshi's Island 3 that the player will notice is the presence of the rotating platform. Like most moving targets, the rotating platform has a moderately small target width that is constantly moving; this presents a challenge in which the player has a small window of time before the platform he's targeting goes out of reach. This is the standard challenge of the level: a rotating platform which, when timed properly, allows Mario to walk off onto the next platform instead of jumping.

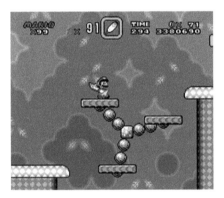

As you can see here, the jump to this platform goes from delta-height-0/d-distance-0 to delta-height four/d-distance-three in just a couple of seconds. Neither of these is a very hard jump, but the second position is, relatively speaking, a lot harder than the first. Thus, although the challenge is easy when attempted the right way, it's still a challenge the player can fail and lose a life on. Note that the reason that these rotating platforms have three arms is so that if a player misses their window of opportunity to jump easily, all they have to do is wait for the next arm to come around—it won't be long. Later in the theme, there will only be one arm on these platforms which makes nailing the timing more important.

Donut Plains 3 also introduces another moving target: the tracked platform. Tracked platforms are another form of moving target, named for the visible tracks that they ride along. These platforms come in two distinct types: the cycling tracked platform and the linear tracked platform.

The cycling tracked platform is the one that appears first in this level: on the left, above we see a platform on a looped track that goes around in endless circles. There are some key differences between the tracked platform and rotating three-armed platform, but technically they're both versions of the same standard challenge that asks the player to wait. The tracked platform lacks three arms, and so the waiting period for a timed jump might be greater. By itself, the rotating tracked platform would be a mutation since it's only qualitatively different from the three-armed platform. Since this challenge connects directly to the three-armed platform, it's an evolution that combines two qualitatively different things into one task.

The important part of this level is the three challenges that come in the middle. The first and simplest is an expansion challenge which increases the d-distance between platforms, making the player perform some real jumps. After this, we see two evolutions that diverge from challenge two.

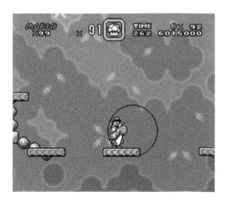

Notice that we're not straying too far from the original idea; only a few variables change whether they're quantitative or qualitative. The biggest change is in the introduction of the toggle switch. This is an inversion of the first evolution, in which the ground is moving and the target is stationary—although it requires the same timing jump skill.

Next, the level adds periodic enemies. This is another simple evolution upon challenge two, in which the designers simply add one new element—the Fuzzy. This is the most common crossover for the moving targets theme, in which an enemy with a small period is placed in the way of a moving platform.

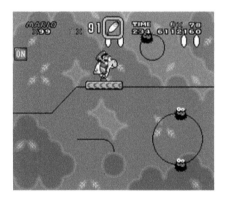

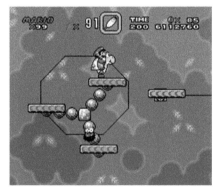

In the next challenge (middle), the Fuzzy shares a track with a platform, essentially modifying challenge two again. This time though, the challenge also includes the linear track from challenge immediately previous with no break in between. Thus, the challenge is essentially A+B, both evolving and expanding from those two challenges. The final challenge (pictured on the right) is actually a step down from this, as is common. The hardest challenge in a level is often not its final challenge. This challenge simply evolves challenge two, with smaller d-distances between the three-armed platform and the linear track.

It seems like a simple level, and it certainly isn't very challenging, but the designers are actually doing quite a lot in Donut Plains 3. This level has done very well in laying the ground work for timing jumps, which is good, because there is a spot-check coming for the timing jump skill in the next castle.

Morton's Castle

The second castle is, in a sense, the last stand of the "waiting game" that the player has had to work through so far. Although the timing jump remains the central skill throughout the rest of the theme, levels after this castle will progressively reduce Mario's ability to wait. To segue into this, this castle does a couple of very interesting things on a broad scale, which we'll address before we dissect the particulars. First, it's worth noting that the castle does not begin with the moving targets theme, but rather its complement, the periodic enemies theme.

For an in-depth analysis of these challenges, you can see the survey of the periodic enemies' skill theme, which also covers this level. Levels occasionally focus on more than one theme in a substantial way, and this is a good example of that. The second part of the castle is, however, very much focused on moving targets with just a few periodic enemies thrown in. Most of the jumps involve these moving platforms, which travel very slowly, testing the player's patience. Most of these jumps carry a zero penalty, meaning that the player merely has to start over if he or she fails that jump. That said, Mario can fall a long way, so the player will quickly become irritated at the slowness of the platforms when doing them over again. It is possible in many spots to complete more than one challenge per cycle of the blocks, and indeed players may attempt it. This is good, because it begins to force players to take their timing jumps quicker—a skill that will be needed later in the game, to be sure—but in a way that isn't yet fatal.

The moving platforms themselves also do two important things that are unusual for the moving targets theme. The first and most obvious difference with these moving platforms is that they can kill Mario. If Mario is caught between the moving block and another solid, he will be crushed and killed instantly. In a sense, this hurts impatient players since they will often get caught in an instant-death situation because they haven't planned/timed correctly. These same platforms, however, have an unusual safety property: they slow down just before final impact. For most of the trip towards their terminals, these moving blocks travel at a steady speed (like everything else in the game). Just before reaching crush-distance, however, they slow down considerably.

While many of the jump events could have a penalty of two, the most common outcome for failing a jump is simply having to start over (penalty zero). Ultimately, the designers thought frustration through repetition and waiting would be enough to push the player to go faster. I think that this was wise; if every fall in this level caused death, new players would hate it and be forced into extreme, slow caution which would be no fun at all.

Now we'll examine the challenges individually; there are actually a number of fairly sly evolutions and expansions in this level. For starters, look at the first screen that establishes the standard challenge. It's actually quite clever in the way that it shows players exactly what is going on, even though they've never seen it before. The right-hand blocks emerge as the left-hand block (on the top of the screen) retracts. This tells the player all of the basic information they need to know about how the level is constructed, with walls that shift positions on a regular timer.

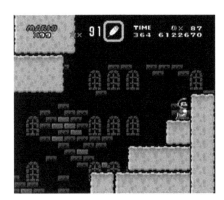

The standard challenge sees quite a few interesting expansions. This section below, for example, is basically the same skill; there are a series of timing jumps to be done with no intercepts or other complications. The real problem here is that while the d-distances have gone down, the platform widths have shrunk, the delta-heights for each jump have increased, and the penalty is now instant death. Nothing has really changed qualitatively, however.

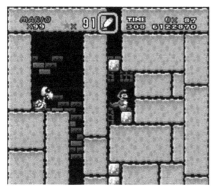 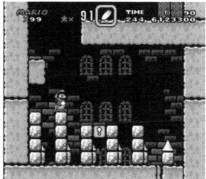

On the right is a different kind of expansion challenge. The delta height for the final bit of this challenge is much higher, and the landings are still quite narrow. The spikes might indicate that the penalty is now one, but really, it's the same danger of fatal crush damage as ever, as those blocks slam into the walls. It also seems like an evolved form of the moving platforms below, but really, the quality of these platforms hasn't changed. Only the amount of space has changed. What's really interesting is that these are definitely the two most exciting challenges in the level, and the precision involved makes a player forget about how this is really just a timing jump in another form.

The goal of the moving targets theme in this level is to force players to learn how to move more quickly and line up several quick jumps in a row, but only timing it once. The designers knew that if the players chose willingly to accelerate their progress by jumping at non-optimal moments, the learning would be less annoying. I have heard many designers say time and again that one of the most important metrics for them when testing a game is finding out "whose fault" a death was. If the player blames him or herself, they'll keep playing because there's clearly something to master. If the player feels that the game is at fault, frustration will result in the play session being over. By goading the players into making the choice to go fast, Castle 2 makes sure that the player will keep coming back to the game through the frustration. It's a very sly technique the designers use here, accomplishing the goal of pushing the player without risking too much frustration because the player knows that, ultimately, they could simply wait and take the easy optimal timing jump.

As a last note, it's worth pointing out that this is one of the few bosses who actually conforms to the skill theme. When Morton Koopa falls from the ceiling, he will stun Mario if both of them are on the ground at the same time. It's not terribly dangerous, but it does employ the timing jump skill that the level has been pounding into the player's brain over and over again. A well-timed jump will save Mario from taking damage and make the boss fight that much easier.

Vanilla Dome 3

The foundation of Vanilla Dome 3 is the expansion challenge. This level contains possibly the best example of how an expansion challenge can be executed in an interesting and consistent way and is one of the better examples of coherence in level design. This level also has a major flaw, but we'll get to that at the end. First, we should start by identifying the standard challenge; it is a very simple jump.

The standard challenge for this level is simply to jump off the platform, then land on it again. The Blarggs force the player to do this with just the right amount of threat. You can see how the consecutive number of these dragons climbs upward. That, of course, is an expansion challenge in which the number of enemies goes up and the space between them goes down. We're not yet at the main course, though. Soon after this, the player will encounter this row of Piranha pipes (left) followed by this moving platform challenge (right). The first instance of the Piranha Pipes is a simple challenge that the player needs to time correctly or use Yoshi to defeat. With the right timing, it's not hard at all, since there's no rush. The platform challenge after this, however, introduces an evolution challenge. Now the player has to get through the Piranha Pipe challenge and stay with the moving platform, a simple A+B evolution challenge. Being removed from the platform like this makes for a kind of abstraction upon the moving targets theme; the target is moving—it's just not accessible! Fortunately, in this case, there's only one moving enemy and one Piranha Pipe. It's easy. The centerpiece of the level is this expansion, which comes later.

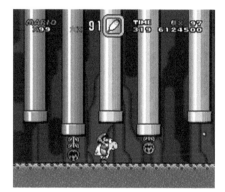

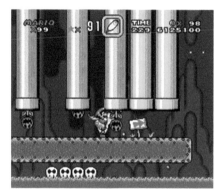

The designers only had to do three things to make this challenge work: lengthen the platform, increase the number of Piranha Pipes, and make sure each one of those pipes is on a different timer. The floating skull platform below takes care of making the challenge sufficiently interesting with no alteration made.

It's not merely the use of obvious expansions upon an A+B evolution that makes this level great, but some other factors that really flush out this level's cleverness. For one thing, we have to consider how well this level mixes moving targets and its complementary theme, periodic enemies. Each one of those Piranha Pipe challenges is built out of a timing/moving targets foundation, but because of those Piranhas, it's also incorporating the periodic enemies theme. There's also this tiny gem of a crossover, which guards the mid-gate.

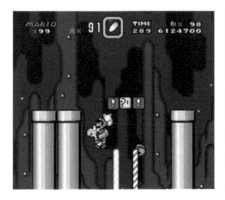 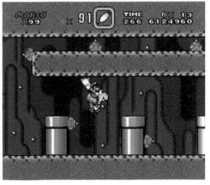

This midgate is guarded by an empty, patrolling shell—it's not easy to drop safely into the gap since the period of the shell's movement is so small; it's probably the fastest periodic enemy in the game. Then there is this section pictured on the right, which features these spike-shells slowly crawling over the geography, many of them in cycles. The skill here, as has been true for a while, is the timing jump. Getting Mario through the patrols requires waiting for the right moment, even if he's going to use Yoshi to eat some of these enemies. After this, the last Piranha/Platform challenge appears. It's a perfect example of a bridge challenge in which the level's main challenges are broken up by a section from the other side of the composite.

Finally, there is a secret extra section in Vanilla Dome 3 that shows us just how many ideas the designers had for this level. The secret section I'm talking about actually comes in Vanilla Dome 4. Vanilla Dome 3 was already getting too long, and so the designers decided that this short-but-challenging section would have to be crammed somewhere in the next level, so they placed at the bottom of a pipe. You can see how obviously it belongs in Vanilla Dome 3, though.

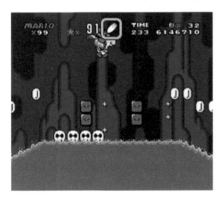 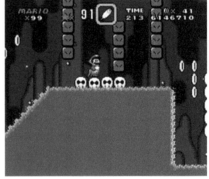

Here we see what the designers really wanted to do: finish their level with this massive barrage of evolution/expansion challenges upon the separation theme. Because the level was already artistically complete (finishing, as it did, with the Piranha Pipe expansion), and because this challenge was significantly harder than what came before, they decided they'd put it in a spot where the player might not even find it. It's too bad really because this last challenge solves the level's one flaw. Vanilla Dome 3 is too easy and too slow. Yes, the challenges lay out in a pleasing, logical fashion. Yes, the level is a stunning example of elegant composite design. The platform is too slow and the challenges are too easy. This secret addition in Vanilla Dome 4, with its many jumps of delta height five or greater, would have given the level the development it deserved.

Cheese Bridge

The Cheese Bridge is a bit of an oddity as a level. Thematically, it really ought to be labeled a moving targets level because almost all of the targets of Mario's jumps are moving. When you start to break it down into its components, however, the truth that emerges is stranger than this. The first section of Cheese Bridge is the part that is most definitely in the moving targets theme—and yet we see no periodic enemies. Rather, the player is met by intercepts, which are the complementary theme to the preservation of momentum theme. This is a great example of how those of us who study games can look back and know that designers weren't obeying hard-and-fast rules, but rather experimenting frequently, and simply keeping those levels, mechanics, and situations that worked the best. In the case of Cheese Bridge, the designers had an idea they wanted to use, and as it turned out, the idea worked very well despite being outside the inter-level pattern.

The three platforms that make up the first part of the level can be activated at different times depending on the player's actions, and so there's no way to measure the "real" delta-heights or d-distances. Moreover, the vertical and (relative) horizontal positions of the platforms change often. The designers did, however, come up with something clever here to make the experience coherent. The first part of the level is designed to accelerate the player's timing jumps. This should not be confused for moving over to the speed side of the skill theme matrix we examined before. Reacting to the oncoming intercepts will prove routinely problematic. Most of the saws come from different sides of the screen, on adjacent tracks, like so. Reacting to one of the saws can easily put Mario in harm's way for the next one.

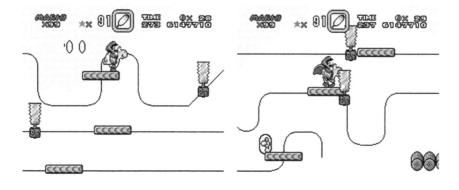

Instead of merely reacting and getting away with it, the player needs to quickly "read" the level design and make a safe plan. There's a lot of data coming at the player—the positions of the platforms and the saws, the velocities of all of those—but the level is wide enough and clear enough that prudent jumps serve the player better than twitchy ones. The speed of the obstacles just accelerates the player's timing jump skills in a fun way.

This level is actually a great example of a series of mutation challenges. Although the shape and position of the platforms changes often, the quantitative distance between them (as well as the number of intercepts) does not change to a particularly significant degree. Essentially, one platform is always safe while the other two are in the path of a saw-blade; these slight qualitative changes (i.e. where the danger is located, relative to the whole group of platforms) are mutations doing what they do best—keeping the game interesting by keeping the tension up, without making the game harder.

As a last note, I want to point out that the first part of this level starts an important trend in the game. Cheese Bridge acts as a kind of mid-point in the game, not numerically, but in terms of development. After this point, the player will face levels that are longer, more challenging and include accumulations (although usually outside of this theme). This level prepares the player with a kind of mid-game training-wheels effect. By accelerating the timing jumps, the designers have made the game harder. By having the platforms all move in relative sync (and stay close together), the player can always make a kind of saving throw after a hasty reaction or poorly-planned timing jump. The feather at the beginning of this level helps a lot with this.

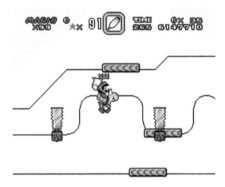

The player here can make a backwards jump and/or use a cape-glide to get back to a platform that was left improperly. In fact, it's not terribly hard in most cases. This introduces players to the harder second "half" of the game that is going to force more mistakes out of newbies. Really, it has to force more mistakes out of the player. The only way a player (rather than a researcher) can know that a game is challenging them at a higher level is they he or she is being forced into more mistakes. The potential for survival after a mistake in Cheese Bridge means that players can have the mistakes and feel the difficulty, but they don't necessarily have to get a game over to prove it. It's not quite training-wheels, but the philosophy behind the design is similar.

The second part of this level tests the same kinds of skills as the first half, but in a different way. This section essentially turns the platform sideways, and forces Mario to hang onto a rope. This rope really does operate like a vertical platform, as Mario can shimmy up and down it instead of moving side to side. The designers did a nice job of introducing this mechanic, coming as abruptly as it does.

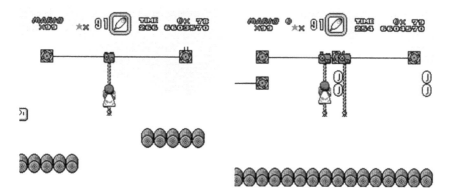

The simple jumps make for an easy introduction, and the coins are placed to encourage vertical movement out of the player. There are a few points in the game where coins indicate a good jump/movement path, but this is almost certainly the best example. (The best example of leading a player with "coins" is certainly the *Donkey Kong Country* series, which does this much more often and with much more elegance. Nevertheless, the idea started with Mario.)

Having adjusted the player to the new mechanic, the level brings in periodic enemies whose complicated and overlapping paths require the player to make quick estimations of the ideal way through. The saw obstacle returns in a different context and with different purpose.

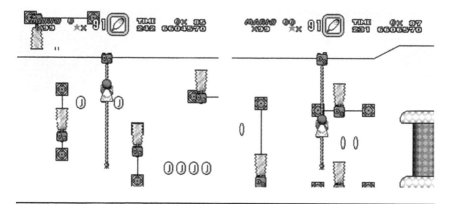

The pattern of evolutions and expansions here is clear: saws start out in vertical parallels and become more dangerous when they run in horizontal parallels. The path suggested by the coins carries over into the first bit, though, to cue the player in on what to do. The saw is rather forgiving because of its deceptively small hitbox, so although new players will be steering very clear of this enemy, this section isn't as dangerous as it seems. Now, this kind of invincible, patrolling enemy and the rope which Mario climbs both strongly suggest the periodic enemies theme. Indeed, you might call this section of the level a gray area that could be placed in the periodic enemies' theme for just this reason. That said, I classify it as a moving targets level because jumping is still so useful. The player ought to have no trouble jumping off the rope and landing back on it to avoid obstacles. This is, in my opinion, just another example of how involved the moving targets theme is with its complement, but it wouldn't be terribly hard to argue that this theme is more like the periodic enemies theme, and that the jumping was just an oversight. The layout of the saws does suggest that jumps weren't intended.

Vanilla Secret 3 & Butter Bridge 1

Vanilla Secret 3 and Butter Bridge represent two of what I call "variations" on the theme of moving targets. I liken these two levels to a fantasia and a toccata. A fantasia generally means that a music composer—or, in our case, a game designer—creates something that's based around spontaneity and improvisation. Of course, this is not the norm in classical music or game design. Well-designed games have a lot of room for a variety of techniques, but if the game, section or level is designed too loosely, it's easy for players to miss the challenge and the fun. (There are a few exceptions, naturally.) In Vanilla Secret 3, however, the designers just decided to throw some things together with only loose organization and let the player sort it out.

There are some ordinary, cycling platforms that stay in place in this level. That, however, is not the fun part. What you see on the right is these waves of dolphins that move in a kind of sine wave shape across the screen. These platforms are so clustered it's that there's no clear optimal path. Instead, the player has to improvise.

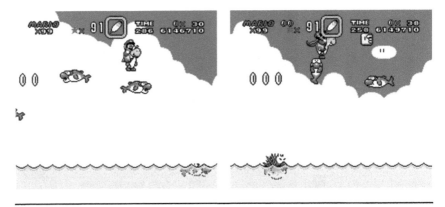

There's also barely any penalty. The puffer fish that lurks in the water is technically dangerous but it's easy to avoid even in the water. Then of course there's all the water; this takes the penalty out of the jumps in the same way it did in the early Yoshi's Island levels. Falling has only a small risk of damage, and little risk of dying. This level is also one of the shortest in the game, in terms of the number of identifiable challenges. There's not a whole lot between Mario and the end-goal, except a lot of room to improvise.

Sticking with the musical metaphor for a moment, we examine the level which is more like a toccata: Butter Bridge 1. A toccata is a musical piece designed to show off an instrumentalist's skill. A toccata can be beautiful, but the first goal of such a piece is to allow the performer to display technical skill in flashy, obvious ways. (Subtle flourishes may also be included, but they aren't the point.) To achieve this sense of flashiness, the toccata will often include things that are obviously difficult, unusual, and sustained. This is the perfect description of Butter Bridge 1.

The first thing the player will notice about Butter Bridge 1 is that the scrolling camera controls the pace of the level. This makes it easy for the designers to force waiting periods and precisely timed jumps, which fit with the current skill theme. What it does not do, however, is make this process easy. The slowly-scrolling camera forces the player to wait, but the tipping-scale platforms in this level make waiting deadly, and this is to say nothing of the fact that all of them have a width of only two blocks.

The platforms sink at a rake of about one coin-block per 15 frames, with a corresponding rise in the platform that makes up the other end of the scale. The tricky part about this is that not only does the filled platform sink, but the opposite platform rises, meaning that for every 15 frames that Mario occupies one of these platforms, the delta-height of the next jump increases by two. Considering that the camera may not always reveal the platform yet to come, this configuration can quickly put Mario in a position he cannot escape. When not occupied, the platforms will return to an even position, but at a rate of about 40 frames per one coin-block—much slower than the damage is done (although if the platform has sunk less than 1/10 of a block, it seems to reset more quickly).

The tipping-scale platforms are unique in *Super Mario World*, but are not the level's only curiosity. At a larger structural level, we encounter another bit of strangeness which fits the toccata metaphor: most of the challenges in this level come in an unbroken chain. Whereas a typical level breaks up its expansions and evolutions with empty platforms, punctuating challenges, or even crossover challenges, Butter Bridge 1 simply puts all of its challenges in a row, such as this monster:

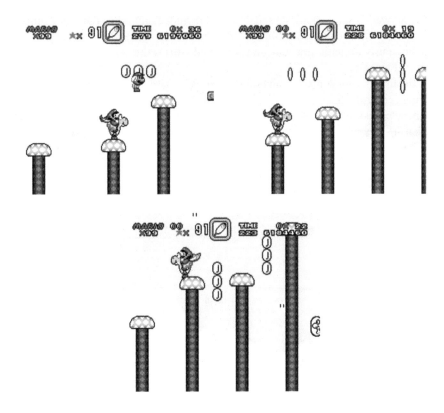

The difference in height means this is an expansion. The fact that the player has no break seems like it should be an evolution, but this is one place in the game where this classification system falls down. This part of the level doesn't look or act like anything else in the game, really, and the sustained action makes the level seem considerably harder than it really is; all the player really needs to do is repeatedly jump and cape-glide back down without changing platforms. The platforms' return to equilibrium is not fast enough to preserve equilibrium indefinitely, but a player constantly jumping and gliding back down will avoid problems. Jumping between the two platforms while gliding can accomplish this even better, while waiting for the screen to scroll. As noted, though, the level gets much easier after a few playthroughs. This is where the toccata comparison is most telling. A toccata displays the performer's talent by sustaining odd and challenging musical passages at unusual length. This, Butter Bridge 1 does. What Butter Bridge does not do, however, is impress an audience. After a few playthroughs, the player will master the skills for the level and it will be easy; it will also look easy. After all, the d-distances between platforms are rarely more than three blocks. There are occasional periodic enemies patrolling between jumps, but they often make the jumps easier because the player can bounce Mario off of them, shortening the only two jumps in the level that are wider-than-normal expansions. There's nothing visually impressive about it, for all its initial acrobatic terror.

Although many of us who have played this level remember it for the second-by-second frustration it gave us, Butter Bridge 1 is one of the shortest levels in the game by total lateral distance, and none of the jumps are particularly far in either direction if the tipping scale mechanic is handled correctly. Mastery of this level, however, looks and feels impressive even to the player who has realized just how easy it really is. A good game cannot always tell players how much they have to learn; sometimes it's necessary for the game to tell them how far they have come.

Forest Secret Area

Forest Secret Area doesn't do that much in the way of a cadence although it's very clearly a moving targets level. What's here is cleverly organized along thematic lines, just not in a real cadence—but the themes are so stunningly clear here that it almost justifies the lack. The only problem is that it's way too easy for the player to break that organization and never see the thematic appropriateness behind it. You might say that this level is art for the artist's sake, which is always a questionable decision. Nevertheless, there's a lot to learn from it as long as we're studying game design. The level contains two platforms at the beginning: front and back. The choice of platforms gives the player subtly different experiences, assuming the player rides only one for the whole way to the goal. The front platform will take Mario through a series of lateral encounters with intercepts with an emphasis on action solutions. In these two spots pictured below, the approaching Wing Koopas will almost pin Mario down beneath the coin-blocks, making his jump haphazard or simply interrupted.

The easiest solution to this is to use fireballs to knock out the oncoming Wing Koopas in one shot, and coincidentally enough, this path takes Mario past a block which will grant one. The thematic material is obvious: this is the intercepts theme at its most action-oriented. I can't see why this is plugged into a moving targets level where it's so easily overlooked, but the designers took a risk here and it didn't go horribly, at least.

The back platform, if ridden the whole way, will still encounter intercepts, but will emphasize jumping solutions and provides a feather powerup. Note that I call them intercepts because the player is, in a sense, in a continuous jump as the platform moves up and down. The effect isn't particularly challenging, but it does simulate intercept-like situations, even if the enemies don't fit the strictest definition.

You can see how, as the platform rises into these Koopas, Mario is forced into an off-platform jump and glide, most likely a back-jump and possibly an enemy bounce. In the first case, the period of the enemies is essentially non-existent (if they turn around, it happens off-screen), but their quantity forces Mario to jump somewhere clear of them: off the platform. The second challenge is a kind of insidious mutation of this: there's only one Wing Koopa but he's on a very short patrol and so has a similar effect.

Both platforms take Mario through this L-shaped intercept trap, but their approach angles make a lot of difference. The fire-flower path takes Mario up into them, revealing the three laterally-flying Wing Koopas first, and offering a clear shot at them with fireballs.

The feather platform path brings Mario in from overhead, offering a shot at jumping on the vertical Wing Koopa before descending with a glide onto (or past) the other three.

The thematic material in this level is delivered so elegantly, so it's a shame that the level's two-platform style makes it so the player will probably never perceive this elegance. The intersections of the platform can't help but suggest a transfer from one platform to another. After all, most of the game's content is delivered as Mario hopping from one platform to another. But only by ignoring this impulse (and perhaps playing the level twice in sequence) can the player actually get the most coherent experience of the level. It's just not likely.

Roy's Castle

Roy's Castle is an interesting take on the tracked content idea from the two bridge levels the player has faced so far. Like Butter Bridge, this level is actually quite short, but because it introduces a mechanic not yet seen in the game, it seems much more difficult at first than it really is. Mario is forced to ride what might be called a caterpillar platform. The platform moves, but does not carry Mario with it, so the player needs to constantly walk Mario along the length of it in order to stay above the lava below. The challenge lies in the fact that this platform takes many different shapes and moves in many different directions. The unpredictability of the first few attempts makes it seem hard—but ultimately there are only really four challenges while on the caterpillar platform, and none of them are particularly complex.

Before we examine the challenges individually, however, it's important to point out three level-wide design considerations. Most of the d-distance for this level is over lava, and so most of the missed jumps will be fatal. There's also no mid-gate, so all failures will result in the player having to completely re-attempt the level. Finally, there's a very important shift in skills that's taking place in this level. Up until now, the core skill of the moving targets theme has been the timing jump. That's still true, but before Roy's Castle, this skill was typically supported by the cape-glide and the back-jump (sometimes both together). In other words, players could afford to make more mistakes than they can in this castle because skilled use of the cape could allow players to recover. Since Cheese Bridge, that recovery has been getting harder and harder, and now this castle completely negates that ability because the caterpillar platform travels very quickly and often in erratic paths. Cape gliding will only result in a stranded, doomed Mario slowly gliding into lava. Back-jumping is basically impossible unless the player has the platform's path completely memorized, and if that's the case, why do they need a back-jump at all? What replaces these skills is the controlled-height jump, which is going to feature more and more prominently as the moving targets theme (and the game as a whole) reaches its climax.

The first challenge sees the platform contract and change shape, taking the form of a staircase. The difficulty lies in the fact that until this challenge the platform had moved in a quick but mostly straight path so that Mario could just walk. Simply walking with the platform is the standard challenge for the level. Now, though, Mario has to jump, although he is faced with two complications. The first complication is that the bottom step of these stairs is always disappearing because of the platform's constant movement. The second complication is that because of the stair shape, half the platform's width is now of no use to him. Essentially, the platform has gotten smaller and changed shape, forcing a timed jump.

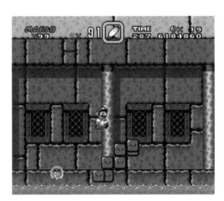

The next challenge is different, and involves no jumping, but is still tricky. The platform bends around several times.

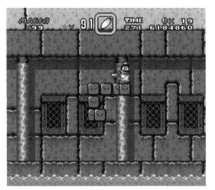 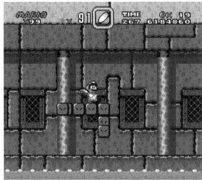

In this case, the player is being tempted to simply overrun the platform. The platform will extend 11 blocks straight out—a distance that the player is intuitively used to by now. The player will be tempted to go into a full run on those 11 blocks, but the platform turns immediately downward resulting in a pitfall. What the designers are doing here is to manipulate the player's most important skill in this skill theme: prediction. The timing jump—the core skill of this theme—involves predicting regular motion. This platform, unlike all that have come before it, is not regular in the same sense the others have been. The skill betrays the player until a few deaths have made him or her cautious.

Next, we see another staircase challenge, although a bit longer. This staircase comes with a typical evolution challenge: add a periodic enemy to a timed jump. These four bouncing fireballs are almost an intercept in that they cause the player to modify Mario's jump-path. But the player is still going to be using periodic enemy skills in predicting the path of this undefeatable obstacle—walking rather than jumping. The designers already introduced the fireball in a kind of warning-shot display, as one of them coasted by the player, revealing its bounce-properties earlier in the level.

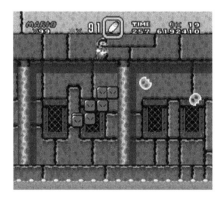

With this knowledge, the player is going to have to guess where these new, dangerous fireballs will bounce, and at what angle. It's not a test of reflexes, but one of prediction. Fortunately, the fireballs aren't very fast, although that doesn't help much when they're being reflected back and forth between ceiling and platform every second.

One interesting note, much like the falling spikes which will succeed them, the fireballs in this section are not cued by the position of the caterpillar platform. Rather, they are cued by Mario crossing an invisible line. This means that the fireballs can come at meaningfully different times, depending on where Mario is on the platform. The third fireball, in particular, can be reflected off the bottom of the caterpillar platform if Mario is further back on it when he hits the fireball's trigger point. It's not a game-breaking flaw, but it does leave one to wonder what the designers had in mind about the player's probable position.

The caterpillar ride ends with a sequence of falling spikes that are complicated by a damaging ceiling and floor. Players who have not been through Vanilla Fortress (a secret level) may not be aware of the falling spike. Whether by coincidence or design, the designers reduced the penalty in this area so that being knocked off the platform—or panicking and falling—would not necessarily be fatal. Mario can still hop back on the platform, although it won't be very easy.

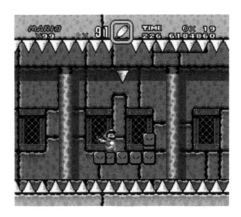

After the initial surprise is gone, these falling spikes aren't altogether so different from Thwomps that the player can't rely on old skills. One complication that we mentioned earlier, though, is that during certain points in the platform's path, the ceiling can be close by. Accordingly, the player has to rely on controlled-height jumps, so Mario doesn't end up in the ceiling spikes, either. Because of all these changes, this section is essentially an inter-level evolution, combining two well-known types of challenge (a moving platform, falling objects) into a single event that requires a skill new to this theme: the controlled-height jump.

Finally, the level closes with a changeover to a kind of moving target not seen for some time: the contracting platform. The basic timed jumps for the contracting platforms are quite simple—indeed, they're from the very beginning of the game. The difficulty comes from the multiple bouncing fireballs that can easily hurt Mario while he's jumping, knocking him into the fatal d-distance. Because of these one might even call this a crossover challenge since the real danger is the periodic fireballs bouncing around the room. Even beyond that, there are some periodic lateral fireballs coming out of Bowser statues.

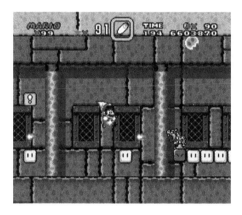

(These fireballs come at regular intervals, making them periodic enemies, although in context they do serve an intercept-like purpose.) The mix takes the challenge we last saw in Yoshi's Island 3 and makes it quite a bit more challenging. The level ends with another stock moving-target boss, albeit with a few token upgrades. Like the next level in the moving targets theme (Chocolate Island 3), the challenges in Roy's Castle really illustrate how much the player has learned and developed over the course of the game. Simple things like moving and contracting platforms have been reimagined in increasingly complex ways.

Chocolate Island 3

Chocolate Island 3 is perhaps the easiest level to explain in the game. The reason for this ease is that it does two very simple things throughout: expansion and evolution. This level is qualitatively very similar to Donut Plains 3; the resemblance is plain in the rotating platforms. Chocolate Island's no longer have three arms, and that's not the only change.

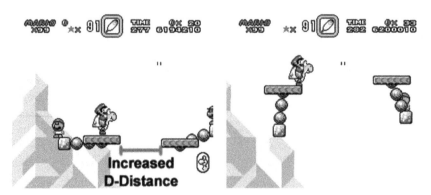

Increased
D-Distance

The differences are clear immediately: Chocolate Island's platforms are much further apart, on average. Specifically, the average d-distance in Donut Plains 3 is 0.9 coin-blocks, which obviously isn't a real length, but is a real average since so many of the d-distances are zero. The average d-distance in Chocolate Island 3 is about 2.1 coin-blocks. That doesn't sound like a huge difference, but one block length matters a lot—especially when the target is moving. To better contextualize this, let's look at the larger jumps. In Chocolate Island 3, there are six jumps with a d-distance of four or greater. In Donut Plains 3, there are none that large. Essentially, the standard challenges for each level are the same, but the expansions for Chocolate Island are much larger. It's a plain and simple numerical upgrade; this doesn't happen often in the game, but it's definitely happening here.

This is to say nothing of the evolution which has swept through the entire level. Every platform hub is now the site of a patrolling periodic enemy that makes the jumps a little bit more difficult. This is just another form of restricting the player's use of the cape-glide. If the player misses the platform jump, they might glide onto the hub block, but they're going to have to bounce off the enemy and then stick the landing all over again. It's not terribly hard, but it is more challenging than if it were merely an empty block. This is a very basic inter-level evolution, where something the player has seen many times before has a new element added to make it more complex.

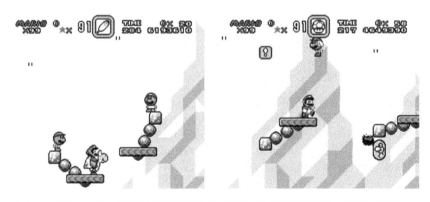

Halfway through the level there's a mutation that exchanges all the Koopas for Fuzzies. These new enemies cover a little bit more ground by circling the hubs and must be avoided rather than defeated. This shortens the window for the timing jump a little bit, but it's not really that much of a change, especially if the player is using Yoshi. The whole point of this, in the end, is that small evolutions and expansions count for a lot. It's easy for amateur designers to feel that their challenges don't "look" sufficiently harder, and so they increase them to what appears correct. But changes that look small can feel big to the player, and that's what matters.

Chocolate Island 4

Chocolate Island 4 forces the player to fight Mario's momentum in a way that is unusual for this game, but fairly typical for previous Mario titles. Additionally—and unusually—it does so in the moving targets theme rather than the preservation of momentum or intercepts themes, where such action is more common. In doing this, the level reclaims some of the literal pitfalls of previous *Super Mario Bros* titles. Mario's ability to stop suddenly and fully shift his momentum is much greater in *Super Mario World* than it was in any of the previous major *Super Mario Bros* titles. By this time in the game, even veterans of the series would have acclimated to the change in game-physics. The slanted platform changes this: because of the slope, Mario can easily fall off this platform while trying to land.

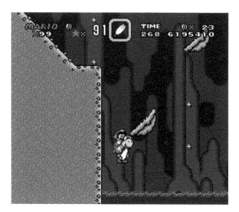

The "sticky" quality of sharp turns still exists, but because of the tendency to fall off one of these platforms, the player can't always focus on the next moving platform. In a sense, this level takes the center of the moving targets theme—precision and timing—and throws a wrench in it by turning the platforms sideways.

This idea doesn't progress very far, possibly because the player can easily catch on and neutralize the disadvantage, especially by landing on the middle and with as little momentum as possible. The standard challenge is, naturally, the first slanted platform. After that the player gets the chance to jump from one slanted platform to another, although there's a platform "safety net" beneath.

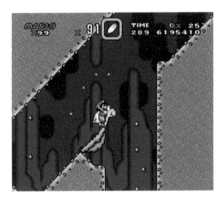
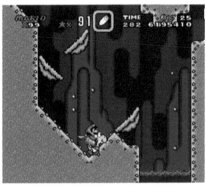

From there, the level's biggest challenge is a large sea of these platforms. The key expansion lies in the two distances that have grown. First, the sea itself is one large pit and so has extended the underlying d-distance (earlier it was four, now it's greater than 15). The individual d-distances between platforms aren't really larger, but now the height between them is greater.

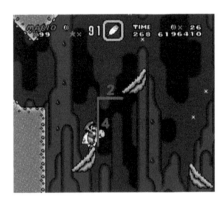
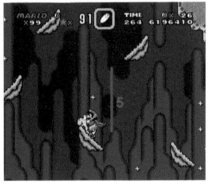

Again, this is really all of the meaningful development that this idea sees. It's a passably distracting break from the standard elements of this skill theme, although it probably could have endured more development, perhaps with some periodic enemies.

The last part of the level worth mentioning for the study of moving targets is the section that contains these three Mega Moles.

It's really a shame that this enemy saw so little development as a platform. Although Valley of Bowser 1 develops the Mega Mole in tunnel combat, their use as possible platforms seems like it could have been greater. (This seems to have been the genesis for the Chomp Rock and Poochy in Yoshi's Island.)

Valley of Bowser 3

Valley of Bowser 3 introduces a peculiar evolution, by adding an expiration timer to its platforms. The level is clearly within the moving targets theme, because it's overflowing with moving targets. These timed platforms are new, and they don't appear anywhere else in the game. Other than that, though, they're very clearly moving targets. On the left, below you can see the standard challenge—almost a training-wheels challenge in the way it has an unlikely penalty. That's good, though, since these platforms are brand new and there's no reason to test the player's attention immediately.

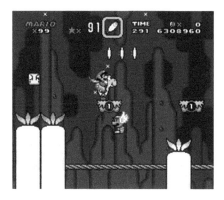 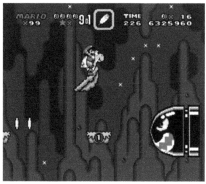

Pictured on the right are a couple of A-to-A evolutions that look like challenges introduced elsewhere in the game, but with timer platforms inserted. Although those are fairly bog-standard, there are some unusual things that keep it interesting. One of those interesting things is a very telling failure, in which the designers try to introduce an accumulation into the theme and don't succeed at all. These slanted platforms exhibit the exact problem mentioned in the intro to this theme: they're not an accumulation but merely an alternative.

Instead of a periodic enemies crossover, elements from the intercepts theme enter the level. These Banzai Bills were not a big threat when we last saw them in Yoshi's Island 2. Ninety percent of the game later, though, they seem quite a bit different, making these jumps more complicated.

This is a great example of how any single element in a videogame can be totally changed by context. The Banzai Bill is an easy enemy with a large hitbox; it's very easy to bounce off in a large arc. This is a problem in Valley of Bowser 3, however, because the platforms here only have a two-block surface area. That large arc can easily put Mario out of range of any platforms. You can see above how, in the second situation, that one small moving platform is the only viable surface after the necessary jump. It's not a pinnacle-level challenge (like some of the ones coming up soon), but it's still tricky because the player will react to the big intercept with a gleeful enemy-bounce and find that the only platform in sight is not where he or she would like it to be.

All in all, the apparent purpose of Valley of Bowser 3 is to sneak in an easy, open level before the onslaught of challenges to come in Castle 7 and Bowser's Castle (or through the Valley Fortress, if the player goes that way). Like the levels to come, it mixes themes in a new and challenging way, and even adds a new kind of evolved moving target, but it's still a relative relief to play after some of the puzzle-based and/or slow levels around it.

Star World 4

Star World 4 is the only level in the Star World that it fits neatly into a skill theme and progresses in a mostly normal way. Unlike Star World 2, it actually does have the kind of variety common to most levels, and unlike Star World 5, it doesn't have a vast free-form section in the middle that makes progression less comprehensible. Star World 4 does something a little unusual, however: it features two different (but thematically linked) standard challenges. This is not the only level that does this, but it isn't a common occurrence. Most of the levels that involve two standard challenges are long enough that both challenges can develop fully. Star World 4 isn't long enough to do that, and so the two standard challenges are abbreviated.

The first standard challenge has Mario jumping from a moving platform onto a stationary platform on which a Koopa is patrolling. The moving platform is a moving target, and the patrolling Koopa (because of the platform edges) is a periodic enemy. In other circumstances this enemy would have been an intercept, but here it's a periodic enemy because the player can see the entire platform before jumping. Instead of having to react, the player has to plan around the enemy's movement and jump at the right time, and that's definitely a skill in the moving targets (rather than intercepts) skill theme.

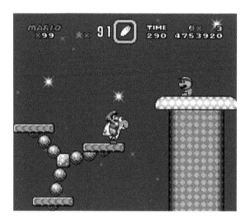

This challenge actually doesn't evolve or expand much until the end of the level, but it may not really need to. Of all the levels in the moving targets theme, this level has the second-highest average delta height (2.7) and d-distance (3.1). Those numbers aren't anything to write home about in and of themselves, but they do show that the gaps between jumps are bigger here than any other level except one. (Note that the level with the highest d-distance is actually Castle #2, which shows that the levels with the most difficult "numbers" don't come late in the game like you would necessarily expect.) This is a kind of consolation that exchanges raw distance for development, since the Star Road levels are short.

There are only two instances of significant development of this standard challenge. The first is pictured just below.

This is an obvious expansion of the standard challenge that doubles the number of periodic enemies on the platform. There is one more expansion which caps the development of this idea, later in the level. This other expansion takes the alternate route; instead of increasing the number of Koopas it contracts the width of the platform.

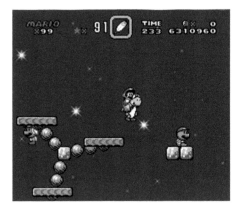

The idea behind both of these challenges is that the player has to choose the appropriate window of time to jump from the moving platform onto the moving enemy (or around it). As the number of enemies goes up or the platform size decreases, it becomes a little trickier to find the right moment before either the platform or enemy winds up at an inconvenient position.

The other challenge in the level that sees regular (if limited) development is a wall of Wing Koopas. Jumping over a dangerous object is the most common activity in any Mario game. This is one of the rare examples (outside of a castle level) where the player is much better off jumping under the dangerous object.

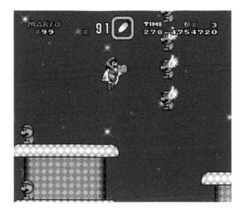

With a cape-glide or by knocking out the bottom Koopa, this isn't too hard a jump. At the apex of their patrol, the Wing Koopas allow eight blocks of height for Mario to jump to the next platform. Later in the level, the amount of space is reduced in a classic expansion-by-contraction.

For this challenge, the peak height of the Wing Koopas is reduced to six blocks above Mario's feet. This isn't the most difficult controlled-height jump in the game by a long shot, but because of the d-distance involved, the player will have to peak Mario's arc before the wall of Koopas, or else take the time to eliminate them all with action techniques.

There is a fairly original take on moving targets challenges in the level that doesn't develop. This challenge involves putting Wing Koopa patrol paths right inside the radius of a rotating platform. It happens twice (the first time is in the contraction above), but it doesn't really go anywhere.

It's a shame this doesn't easy to add more enemies like this or complicate the shape, but the level never goes through with it, which is unfortunate. This is one of the rare instances in which accumulation might have been concretely possible.

Although there are two different standard challenges which see development in Star World 4, that development is short. The real magic of the level is that these challenges cohere well because the first is in the moving targets theme while the second is clearly in the periodic enemies theme (patrolling Wing Koopas are just that—a patrol). While this is an unusual level, it's only because it uses established patterns in a weird way, rather than breaking those patterns altogether.

Way Cool

Way Cool is the most difficult level in this skill theme, although it's different from the pinnacle levels in other skill themes because it doesn't include an accumulation. What makes Way Cool interesting is how well it fuses the two sides of the genre declension. Although the central skill in this level is definitely the timing jump, there are periodic enemies everywhere in the level. These enemies are set in a great variety of challenging loops, sometimes by shape and sometimes sheer density. This is the standard challenge:

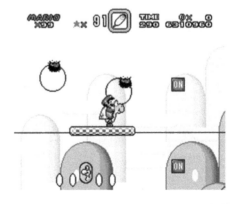

From here, the Fuzzies will only become more challenging, via a variety of evolutions and expansions.

There's an important difference between this level and Cheese Bridge: the moving platform is four blocks wide, rather than the three-block platform from its ancestor. In fact, the vast majority of moving platforms across the entire game have been three blocks wide. This one is four blocks wide because the player is going to need that extra space. Many of the periodic enemies come in pairs, and their heterogeneous periods make jumps complicated. For example, here's an obvious expansion/evolution of the standard challenge.

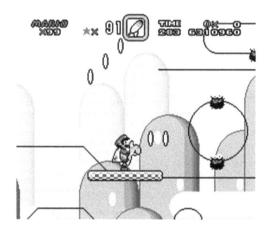

By allowing Mario to back up an extra block length on the moving platform, the designers extended the window of opportunity for making that jump. Additionally, the added width can allow Mario to jump from one side of the platform to the other, which would have been much more difficult in the earlier version of this level.

As one might expect, the designers used inter-level evolutions here too: the on/off switches of Donut Plains 3 are mixed in to devious effect. There is a single ideal path in this level that will lead to the acquisition of Yoshi and an early exit. The player would need quite a bit of good luck to find that path on his or her first try, however, because the switches function counterintuitively. The high road, typically the domain of secrets in Mario games, is actually a giant trap that leads the player back to the beginning. There are several other dead-ends that will result in a disappointingly inexorable death, too. There are also some odd enemy path shapes, and when the saws show up in this level, they aren't telegraphed nearly as far in advance as they are in Cheese Bridge.

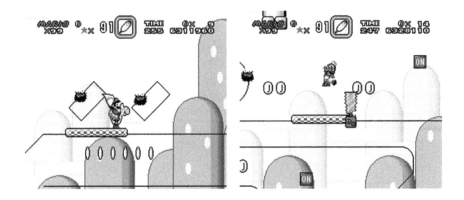

Many of these jumps require very precise timing and a short, quick jump-arc, but none of the jumps goes very far, and no jump ever requires bypassing more than two enemies. This is a big contrast from Valley Fortress or Tubular, where the same challenges just grow larger and larger. The designers really deserve credit for creating challenges with small quirky innovations where brute-force expansion might have been easier.

As was the case in Cheese Bridge, the second half of this level might ordinarily fit into the periodic enemies theme; it certainly uses a lot of them. I think the designers did a nice job straddling the line between the two themes, however, by including a lot of interesting jumps and alternate paths through the level that mix up the challenges. It's possible to survive most of the tracked content—like the standard challenge and its evolution/expansions, below—by going only up and down the rope.

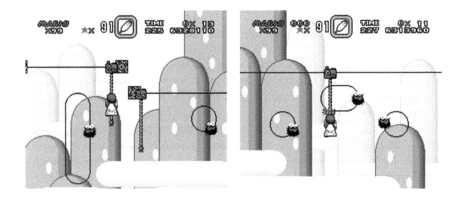

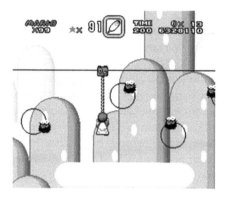

In fact, this would have made for excellent training for Tubular had it come *before* that level since it involves the same essential skill: vertical movement and lots of very precise prediction. The player will probably have to do this section more than once because the path is jam-packed with enemies. Nothing really prepares the player for Tubular, and in the end, this wasn't meant to do so, either. Well-timed jumps from the top of the rope are a viable strategy here—if not essential, considering that the player has never seen periodic enemies like these before. Jumping over the enemies here with a short cape-glide is exactly the strategy used earlier in the level to avoid the same circling enemy traps, so it's no surprise that players might try it again and succeed.

Larry's Castle

The final castle features the only real accumulation in the moving targets theme, although it isn't as well-developed as the accumulations in other themes. This level also serves as a good example of why accumulations are few in this theme, and crossovers so frequent. The standard challenge for the level is remarkable amongst moving targets, especially this late in the game because the penalty is only one.

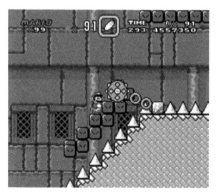 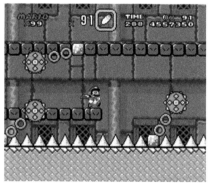

This challenge introduces the centerpiece of this level, an encounter between caterpillar platform and Ball'n'Chain. As the write-up of this theme has explained several times before, the moving targets theme declines frequently and deeply into the periodic enemies theme and this level is no exception. This section is crowded with periodic enemies, but it's still clearly in the moving targets because Mario is always jumping, rather than running. Timed, precise running is the hallmark of the periodic enemies theme, but the player doesn't have time to pause and run between all the Ball'n'Chains in this level. The caterpillar platform Mario is standing on will simply leave him behind. Instead, the best course is to jump at the right moment and keep moving forward with the platform.

The standard challenge first expands, and then evolves. The most obvious change is the expansion that raises the penalty from one to two, moving from spikes to lava.

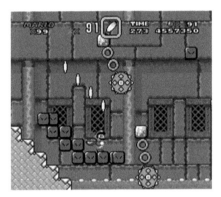 

Later, there is an evolution/expansion when the platform begins tracking around the Ball'n'Chain in a tight square shape, a form that is not only qualitatively more complex, but also a contraction that greatly reduces the surface area of the platform. Neither of these are proper accumulations, however. The real moment of accumulation is quite brief and would be unremarkable, except that it's the only example in the theme.

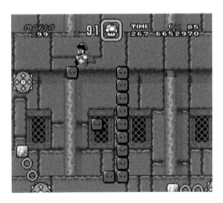 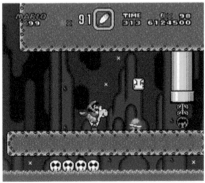

Here, the level combines the caterpillar platform's movement properties with an element from Vanilla Dome 3. In that earlier level, the player had to separate Mario from the platform while still staying close to it (pictured on the right, above). Here, the player has to do the same, although this time the platform moves both vertically and horizontally as the player tracks it. Additionally, the surface area of the starting platforms is the absolute minimum size. The period of separation from the caterpillar platform continues after those first jumps, however.

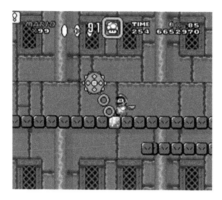

If anything, the separation period gets easier after the first couple of jumps, as Mario can run freely across a stable platform. Still though, the combination of separation and a caterpillar platform is the only real accumulation in the theme, and for one brief instant it was different and interesting. The designers could have done a lot more with it, but at least they found a way to use accumulation in this theme as they did in all the other themes.

The second half of the level is fully in the periodic enemies declension but is not covered in Chapter 5 because it's so short. Across a few short challenges, this section introduces a sharpened log, a fireball, and Magikoopa. It then combines each two of them, and then all three at the end.

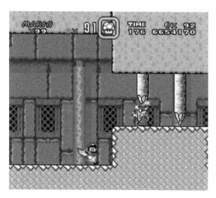 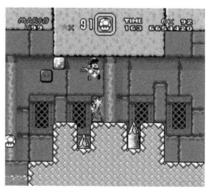

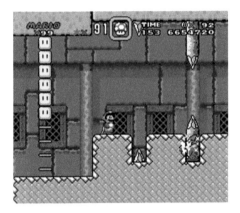

The only thing I hold against this, and why I don't give it its own section, is that it's not clear that the challenges get harder. Only the final bridge challenge is clearly more difficult than what's come before.

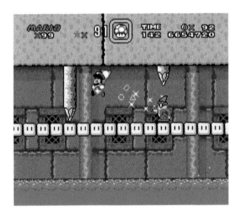

Mario faces all three types of danger in this challenge. This section definitely has the structure of a cadence (specifically the bow cadence I'll talk about in Chapter 10), but it's awfully short, and so I don't think it needs its own entry.

5

The Periodic Enemies Theme

The periodic enemies theme is about enemies that move in predictable, perpetual loops. This is not limited to literal loops; periodic enemies can move back and forth or up and down, as long as that movement is regular and repeating. The "period" of an enemy is the length of time it takes that enemy to complete one of these loops. Additionally, this definition includes "inanimate" enemies like fireballs and sharpened spikes, as long as they exhibit that periodic behavior. The periodic enemies theme is, in a sense, the inverse of the moving targets theme. Where the moving targets theme saw Mario aiming for cycling, patrolling, and otherwise regularly moving platforms, this theme sees him aim his jumps and runs away from cycling, patrolling, and otherwise regularly moving enemies. This makes sense inasmuch as the two themes are complementary. As this book notes many times, *Super Mario World* is a composite of the platforming and action genres, and this skill theme makes use of the action side of the timing idea. This is not to say that this theme completely abandons the platforming genre; a composite game never truly abandons either of its constituent genres. The jumping in this theme is downplayed, and this is reflected in a key stat. The jumps in the periodic enemies theme have the lowest average delta-height of any skill theme. When jumps come in this theme, they're usually small. As in the moving targets theme, this is because the jumps in this theme are about timing rather than momentum. Much of the time Mario doesn't have to jump at all to avoid periodic enemies; instead, he only needs to run at the right moment.

The periodic enemies theme is in the action declension not because there is a great deal of combat (as there is in the intercepts theme) but because the player is often forced to do a non-combat task common to action games: precise movement. Consider that Galaga, Golden Axe, and Prince of Persia all have in common the need for the player to steer their avatar around enemy obstacles, precisely. Even though combat is an option in those games—and indeed the most prominent option in some of them—the player's success also depends on evasion and timing. This is what the player has to do much of the time in the periodic enemies theme in *Super Mario World*. The theme isolates non-jump movement by use of terrain and the second-most important property of most periodic enemies.

The pathways above both make jumping more difficult than walking. Both also feature periodic enemies that are invincible (the Ball'n'Chain). That invincibility is a key part of the periodic enemies theme in that it completely eliminates combat solutions. Given that, this is the theme that requires the greatest precision in how the player controls Mario. That doesn't make this theme the hardest theme, however. Usually, the player has lots of time to figure out how to approach problems in this theme and does not need great reflexes to get through them.

Most, but not all, of the periodic enemies levels are castle or fortress levels. The iteration that occurs across these levels is to take a look at the illustrations of the first three levels, specifically paying attention to the way each new periodic enemy attacks.

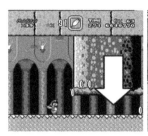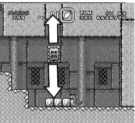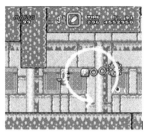

The first castle introduces the smashing pillar, which is only dangerous in one direction. The second castle introduces fireballs and Whomps, which are dangerous because they go up and down, as well as Dry Bones, which are dangerous in side-to-side patrols. Vanilla Fortress, the third periodic enemies level, introduces the Ball'n'Chain, which swings in circles. (Technically, the second castle introduces the Ball'n'Chain briefly, but it doesn't introduce any evolutions or expansion on the idea until Vanilla Fortress.) Each iterated periodic shape is a little bit more complex and more dangerous than the last. The fourth castle introduces the first accumulation, where up/down periodic enemies meet the down-only spiked ceiling.

After this, the game alternates introducing new challenge types and then including them in an accumulation. Forest of Illusion 2 introduces enemies on box-shaped paths, and Forest Fortress includes them in an (evolved) accumulation with both box-shaped paths and one-directional smashers.

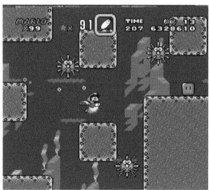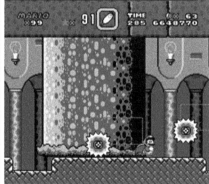

Chocolate Fortress likewise introduces the retracting spike obstacle, while the sixth castle evolves this obstacle and stacks it up with the box-shaped patrols from earlier.

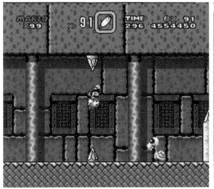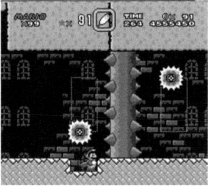

In both of these accumulations, there's a clear evolution in which one element is added to another (the very common "A+B" evolution.) That said, the accumulated material never gets beyond two types of periodic enemy in a level at a time. Even in the hardest single challenge in the theme, there are only two kinds of periodic enemies stacked up at once.

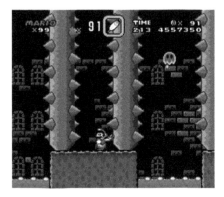

This isn't a flaw or an oversight; Valley Fortress is exactly as difficult as it needs to be. The central skill of this theme is timing, and when periodic enemies that move at two different speeds stack up, the player must be precise to succeed at the timing jump. We know that two enemies with two different periods can make for a great challenge because that happens a lot in the accumulations of this theme. Would three heterogeneous periods have been too much for the player? It's hard to say, but it's not hard to imagine how the designers might have had a difficult time coordinating three periodic enemies. In any case, the two-period challenges of this theme are so well executed that the absence of three-period challenges isn't detrimental to the game.

Iggy's Castle

Because this theme begins in a Castle, there are no proper training-wheels challenges. The first level, however, is far easier than others in the theme, even if it doesn't fit the mold of a typical training-wheels challenge. What makes this level easier (and centers it in the periodic enemies theme) is this grating that is placed all over the first section of the level.

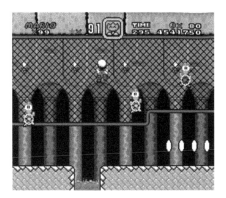 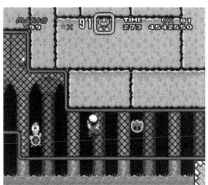

This grating, which is one of the rarest features in the game (appearing only one other time), allows the player complete control over Mario's motion. All of the normal vector problems that might affect Mario on dry levels or in water are gone. While he climbs the mesh, Mario moves at the exact same speed in every direction, but only when the player wants him to do so. Gravity does not pull on him, nor does a balloon effect force him upwards. Even though there are Koopas climbing on the same mesh that can theoretically damage him, it's extremely easy to avoid them. It's a useful introduction to periodic enemies, however, in that many of these Koopas and the fireball seen in the screenshots above are looping periodically; they just have abnormally long periods. Rather than force the player to execute a timing jump through these enemies, the player can simply climb at a steady pace through the slow, highly-predictable loop. The Koopas do a good job of emphasizing the action part of the level, but it's quite easy to defeat them. Of course, there is a penalty that Mario can incur if he falls, but it's so unlikely that this is almost a training-wheels challenge throughout.

The second part of the level is much the same, teaching the player how to deal with periodic enemies while reducing the likelihood of real danger. The giant smashing pillar that descends from the ceiling could damage Mario, but won't often do so because its period is so long and the safe spots are so obvious. It's more likely that the player would get caught under these than get hit by the Koopas of the previous section, but it's not that much more likely. The smashers aren't fast, but once they start firing, they have to cover a lot of distance before they actually reach Mario.

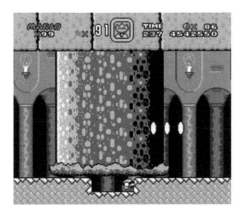

Like most of the large, dangerous objects in the game, they also telegraph their motion. In the end, however, they're just a typical example of the kind of periodic hazard that will inhabit many castles: an invulnerable source of damage on a repeating loop.

As a last bit of evidence that this level is designed to be extra easy, consider that it has essentially no evolution or expansion challenges. The nearest thing to either evolution or expansion is here, where the pit is between the smash-zone and the safe part of the level.

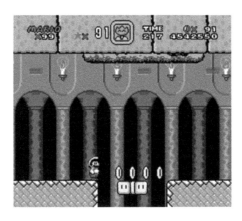

As you can see, this isn't much of an evolution or expansion since the gap is still small and bridged by a contracting platform. It does make for a short, quasi-crossover challenge since we have a moving target, but it's so simple and avoidable that it doesn't add much to the level.

Morton's Castle (First Section)

The second castle begins with one of the most typical examples of the periodic enemies theme, although the level switches themes halfway through to the moving targets theme (which we've already covered in Chapter 4). This makes sense inasmuch as the two are complements and it's easy for the designers to slide from one to another. No skill theme ever completely abandons either of the composite genres. Every periodic enemies theme contains a little of the moving targets theme, and vice versa; that's part of what makes a composite game coherent. Let's take a look at the examples so we can see the specifics of what this means.

The goal of the first section of the castle is to focus the player on pure timing, eschewing even the timing jump in favor of a timing run. Invulnerability is a typical property of periodic enemies, especially in castles, and this one is no exception; the Thwomps and Ball'n'Chain enemies are all invulnerable. There's another property that appears here, and it is a little more complicated: When dealing with periodic enemies, it's often easier *not* to jump. The beginning of this castle is a great example of how this can be so.

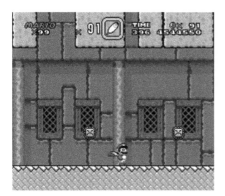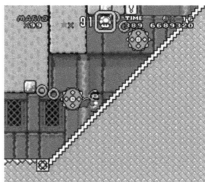

Seeing these Thwimps, it's easy for the player to simply try to jump over them. Doing so will cause Mario to take damage most of the time. The arc of this enemy's movement cuts across Mario's forward jump arc in an uncommonly steep path, and these enemies also move up and down through the air much faster than Mario can jump. (Remember to ignore everything you know about physics.) Instead of jumping, the best thing the player can do is simply time the jump of the Thwimps and have Mario walk underneath them. The same goes for the Ball'n'Chains that follow these Thwimps; the escalator stairs might trick the player into thinking that it's time to ramp up Mario's momentum, but it isn't so. Because of the angle of the ramp, Mario would have to squeeze through a space only one or two blocks wide at the peak of his jump. Instead, the player is better off just running through the gauntlet of obstacles at the right moment, even if it means fighting the momentum of the escalator a little bit.

The second section starts moving back toward the platforming declension but sticks with the focus on periodic enemies. The Thwomps are the best example of this.

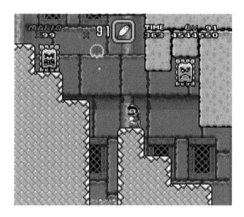

Notice that Mario is jumping, and the player has to use precise timing, but it's not quite a platforming challenge. Mario is going under the Thwomps (and even possibly the fireball), not above them. Fast-reaction jumps or long distance-jumps are not the best way to survive this gauntlet; small jumps and well-timed runs are. Just as before, this section is another typical example of the kind of action we'll see throughout the periodic enemies theme. Just as before, there aren't many evolutions or expansions yet. Plenty of those will show up later.

Vanilla Fortress

Vanilla Fortress, the only water-based castle level, is full of interesting challenges from a game designer's point of view. From the perspective of a player, however, these challenges are perhaps a bit annoying because of how slow they are. What the designer loves, but the player probably doesn't sense, is the elegance of these challenges. Consider the first stretch in which the player has to steer Mario through a gauntlet of swinging maces, through which we have these Fishbones swimming:

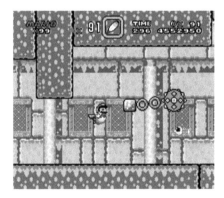

This is a wonderful example of a mutation challenge, one of the best in the game, because it captures exactly what a mutation challenge is about. In every case here, Mario is facing one Ball'n'Chain and one Fishbones, but their relative positions are different. The images above show how Mario's movements change slightly—always in a different direction through a differently sized space. The complexity and level of challenge don't change, but the *feel* of the challenges does. Because of the odd way that swimming works, swimming upwards to shoot the gap between the mace-head and the fish (as you see in the first screenshot) is a different skill than controlling Mario's plummet to the right height (as you see in the second). This is one of the best examples of a qualitative change without any increase in complexity or difficulty. Is it fun? Not especially. This level is a little bit slow and tedious, except for the last section. Not everything that interests a designer is fun for the player. This is a lesson we'll see several times in this book.

The other point of excellence in this level is how nicely it begins the player's training in the way of controlled-height jumps. Water levels are generally considered less fun than dry levels, a judgment I agree with, but they do accomplish one thing well, and that is to teach one of the game's most difficult skills. The controlled-height jump is any jump in which Mario has to go below his maximum possible height or otherwise face a serious risk of damage. Players are habituated to maximum height jumps, as it allows the most time for adjustments before landing. There are many controlled-height jumps to come in Valley of Bowser and the Special zone, but the training begins here.

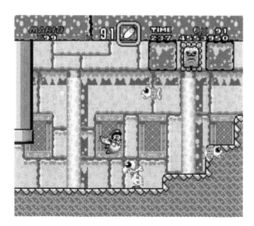

You can see in this evolution/expansion how Mario has to carefully thread his way through enemies that can all move fast, relative to his own swimming. The Dry Bones and Fishbones both force Mario to move, but gaining height isn't an option because of the speed of the Thwomp he must eventually pass.

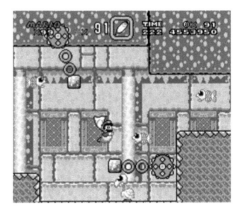

The pinnacle challenge for the level is this evolution/expansion that combines most of the level's contents into one dangerous cluster. The near-overlap of the two Ball'n'Chains means that Mario will have to shoot through the challenge rapidly or else lose the window of safety. The other enemies and terrain contract the path that's available during that limited window, forcing Mario's swim motions to be very tight on the vertical axis. This tight vertical motion is not particularly hard when done in the water, but it does help to show the player when a controlled-height jump is necessary, and how a controlled-height jump might be done.

Lemmy's Castle

Lemmy's Castle is firmly in the periodic enemies theme, but it doesn't look like it is. Placement in a skill theme is determined by what skills the player uses, not by appearances. Most of the time, a challenge's appearance will show the player what skills will be necessary, but this is a case where they don't. The first section resembles something that might come out of the intercepts theme, when Magikoopa appears and starts flinging projectiles at Mario. The important thing to notice is how Magikoopa's placement makes a huge difference in how this level's challenges play out.

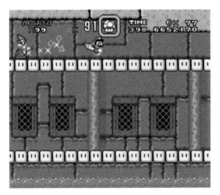
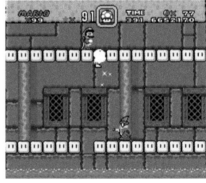

Early in the level, Magikoopa's primary purposes is in opening up safe paths in the blocks. Mario has to stand on the right block and wait for Magikoopa to transform it. Walking to the right spot and waiting is, as we have seen, the defining skill of the periodic enemies theme.

There are rules governing Magikoopa's appearances; he will always prefer to spawn at a different height than Mario, if a platform exists to allow that. He also tends to prefer to appear in front of Mario rather than behind him (although he can do both). Magikoopa's exact position can vary greatly, as there are many different platforms for him to stand on. As such, it's hard to divide the first half of the level into proper challenges. There are obviously three sections to the first half, the section already seen, and the water and lava sections below.

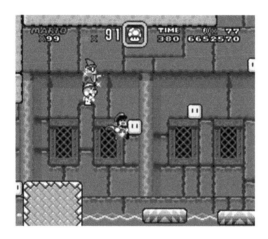

This section is almost reminiscent of a shooter, given how much dodging Mario has to do. Standing in the right place and waiting to move is still the important skill, however. Players who try to run fast usually end up closer to Magikoopa and his projectiles, and thus take damage because he prefers to spawn in front of Mario.

The second half of the level creates an interesting inversion of typical level design. This section of the level is full of moving platforms and very few enemies. That sounds like a description of the moving targets theme, but here, the designers find a way to turn the lava below those platforms into a periodic enemy.

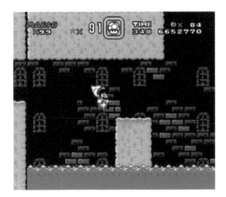
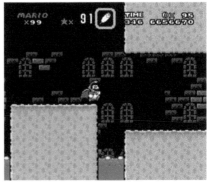

Rather than have the lava surge up and down in the manner of a periodic enemy, the platforms accomplish the same effect by dropping into the lava and emerging from it in a regular, periodic fashion. Although the mechanism is a moving platform, the effect is still one of a periodic enemy. The skill for avoiding death is, accordingly, a timed run (and occasionally, a small jump).

Those platforms are not the only element in the second half, however; there are also numerous Dry Bones and fireballs cast into periodic roles. Many of the challenges featuring these enemies display inverted forms as well. The first enemies Mario encounters are a fireball and a Dry Bones that patrols the platform beyond. The player has to time the jump to get through the heterogeneous periods of the two enemies.

5. The Periodic Enemies Theme

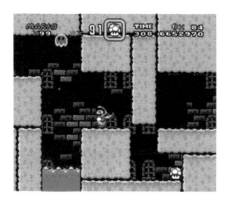

This idea evolves and expands. In the evolution, Mario has to make the same timed jump, but now has to jump upwards, adding positive delta-height. In the second iteration, he descends, but into a contracted space. This pattern of evolution followed by expansion repeats later in the level.

Once again Mario makes an ascending jump, which is an evolution, then makes a descending jump into a space which has undergone expansion-by-contraction. This pattern, of Standard/Evolution/Expansion is one of the most common patterns in *Super Mario World*, but it's a little less common to see that pattern repeated this way, twice in a row.

Ludwig's Castle

Ludwig's castle is interesting because of the connections between its three sections. All three are clearly in the periodic enemies theme, but the mechanic connections between the sections are nebulous. The level starts with a long gauntlet of Ball'n'Chain challenges.

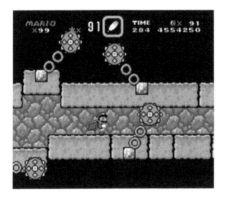 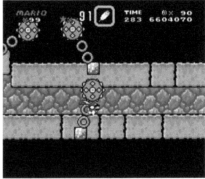

At more than 20 blocks in length, this is the longest ground-based challenge in the game. (There are some longer challenges that involve cape flight.) There is no reliable safe spot in the gauntlet, and there are several places where the player's skills will be stretched. On the right, above, you can see a spot where Mario is forced by the timing of the maces to run and duck. Now, this "slide" technique had been around since the first Super Mario game, and it is very intuitive, but it's new for this skill theme. There are a few more cases later on in the theme where this skill will be tested.

Next, there is a surprising evolution of the ceiling-mounted smashers from the first castle. In this case, the entire ceiling is on a periodic timer that can be reset by a switch in the middle of the area. Without hitting this switch, Mario will be crushed—and there's not much leeway time in getting there. The trick is that going too fast (especially with the cape) will cause Mario to be hurt and probably lose a life because of these fireballs.

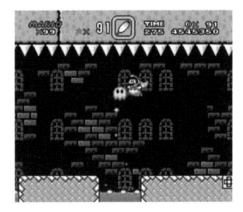

If Mario is running at full momentum, he will almost certainly collide with the fireballs. The player is better off breaking Mario's momentum at the edge of each pit and proceeding just a little bit more slowly. The challenge here is primarily psychological. Waiting to make a jump or a run is totally normal for the periodic enemies theme, but the sinking ceiling can cause the player to rush and take damage from the fireballs or die in the lava pits.

 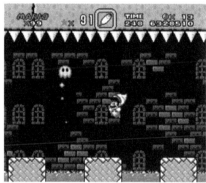

The last section of the castle is yet another manifestation of periodic enemies. The Koopas all move in repeating loops along the only other fence-grating section in the game, the first being in the first castle. Unfortunately, there's virtually nothing interesting to say about this section; the climbable grating is a break from typical platforming, but not one that sees any interesting development.

What is interesting is that this level presents three different kinds of periodic enemies, but barely develops any of them. In the first two sections, we could say that there are one or two iterations of each idea, but that doesn't add up to a cadence. Given that this level arrives after the halfway point of the game, it's strange that it doesn't follow the normal rules of development. There are plenty of levels that are just weird and don't follow any clear organizational pattern; we'll see those in a Chapter 9. This level is clearly in a skill theme, yet it lacks cadence-style organization. Why that happened is anyone's guess.

Forest of Illusion 2

Forest of Illusion 2 is another water level in the periodic enemies theme. If you have read the intercepts theme, you know that most of the water levels are intercept-based. For the most part, this is because the intercept theme fits water so well. Although this level is definitely in the periodic enemies theme, it declines irregularly toward the intercepts theme in a few sections. This is actually a useful object lesson.

The designers could have invented a variety of new kinds of periodic enemy to fill this level with periodic content. They chose not to do so and chose instead to implement an irregular genre crossover. A common problem I notice with young designers is the tendency to design a completely new enemy or environmental feature every time they want to add to a level. This, of course, leads to a lot of design problems and a bloated schedule. Here, we see *Super Mario World*'s designers diverge from the normal pattern of genre crossovers because it makes practical sense. It's important to remember that the skill themes are a pattern and not a rule. The intercept elements in this level work well enough, and sometimes quite well. In short, the lesson here is to not overdesign, no matter the reason.

The main feature and standard challenge of this level is the Urchin, a slow-moving and nearly indestructible enemy that has one of the game's hardest hitboxes. The standard challenge consists of a couple of patrolling Urchins. The next challenge gives us a simple A+B evolution: a wave of water-specific intercepts passes through an evolved version of the standard challenge.

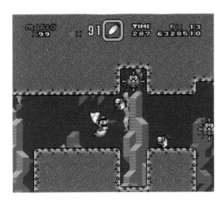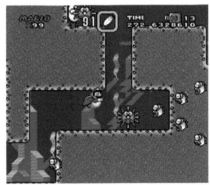

With a cape or fire-flower, there's nothing especially hard about these enemies because they're so slow. That said, the period of the Urchin and the shape of oncoming Blurps both force Mario to slow down. Effectively, this is a signal to the player to start using a periodic enemy mindset and skills instead of rushing, as they might do if this level were in the intercepts theme.

The next significant challenge is the introduction of looping Urchins, a straightforward evolution of the standard Urchin challenge. These looping Urchins always come in groups of more than one, so as to make their overlapping periods a greater challenge. The second challenge below is actually from a little bit later in the level (skipping a couple of unrelated challenges) but is a direct expansion of the first rotating Urchin challenge.

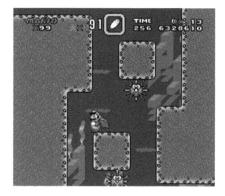 

The pattern is obvious: after the introduction to looping Urchins, there is a simple expansion challenge that features three Urchins rather than two.

There is another evolutionary branch which runs through this level as well. The first A+B evolution later expands and evolves into this challenge.

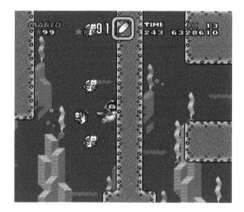

There's still only one Urchin, but now there are more swimming intercepts, and the type of intercept has evolved from the Blurp to the more dangerous Rip Van Fish (RVF). Strangely, this combination does not evolve or expand beyond this point.

The level returns to challenges that focus mainly on the Urchin enemy. The patrols paths of these Urchins are cut progressively shorter so that the player has to shoot Mario through much more quickly than before. This is particularly problematic for the last Urchin, which requires that Mario plunge downwards.

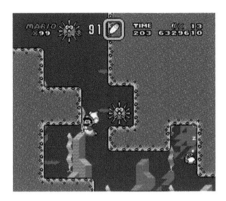

A downward thrusting motion is one of the most counterintuitive in the game, because it's impossible in dry levels. In a water level, though, holding the down button on the directional pad will cause Mario to sink with controllable speed. This isn't the first time the player has had to use this skill, but it's the first time that Mario has had to drop through a periodic enemy patrol into unseen territory. Mechanically, it's like everything in this level: a little bit easy for this point in the game. Psychologically, on the other hand, it's an interesting way of making the player uncomfortable by doing something unfamiliar.

If you believe in that sort of psychological setup as a function of design, then that plunge works well as a setup into the final challenge of the level, which directly evolves the previous challenge by changing the enemy type. Here we see the big crossover into the intercepts theme, as the player is confronted with the rare Alerting Chuck, who summons a swarm of RVFs. The RVF is faster than Mario when travelling laterally, so this challenge is a problem. The mitigating aspect is that it cannot travel in a perfectly horizontal line and will overshoot Mario on the x-axis very often. Because of this, the designers designed cleverly here. By putting almost all the intercepts above Mario, they are more likely to scare the player than to actually make contact with Mario.

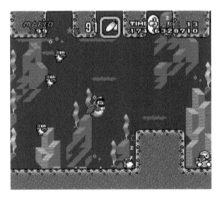

Had half of these fish been located below Mario, the crisscross patterns would have been very dangerous, but because only a couple of them were below, Mario can sink to avoid the bigger swarm above him as he approaches the end-gate. Once again, this is pure psychology. By simply doing what a player would naturally do (shying away from danger), Mario will be able to get to the gate with relative ease, but the sudden shock of seeing all the enemies wake up makes this challenge more exciting.

Forest Fortress

Forest Fortress is as interesting for its flaws as it is for its successes. This isn't to say that it's a bad level. A bad level would be one that is never fun, and this isn't the case with Forest Fortress. The level is fun; it's just designed backwards. The problem comes from the fact that the looping, tracked saws of this fortress have a flaw in their design.

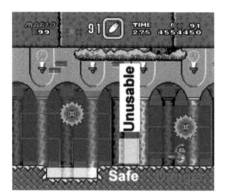 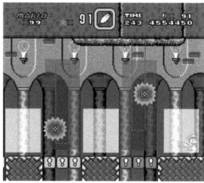

When these saws are tracked along a mostly horizontal path, they are quite difficult for new players. First, the saws are big and therefore harder to avoid, their hit-box is unforgiving, and they deal damage on all sides of the enemy sprite. Secondly, the saws move faster than most enemies, making it harder to time Mario's jump correctly. Third, the saws spend a lot of time in range of Mario, meaning that simply "walking out" of the danger zone is more difficult—most of the safe spots are only one block wide. (Interestingly, though, this is one of the purest examples of the walk-don't-jump aspect of the periodic enemies theme. Jumping will almost always earn Mario a saw to the torso, whereas merely walking with good timing will leave him safe.) Compounding all of these difficulties is the fact that the level scrolls at a set rate, trapping the player in range of these saws. There are also ceiling-smashers that reduce the amount of safe space in each challenge even further.

The reason why this is structurally backwards is because these lateral saws (pictured above, left) are the absolute hardest part of the whole level, and they come first. Once the saws switch to vertical tracks (pictured above, right), they're hardly difficult at all. Even if the player has been negligent in completing the switch palaces, the path of these saws takes them far away from the player, and the length of that path means that the period is long enough for even inexperienced players to avoid the enemy sprite. Because of this discrepancy, the second half of the first section is much easier than the first. Indeed, just about everything in the level is much easier than the first section, but these jumps especially. If this seems inappropriate based on what you might know about how levels in *Super Mario World* have progressed, it is. Normally the lateral saws would be an evolution/expansion of the vertical saws. And it would be a fresh and original evolution that hasn't appeared in the game so far. It's too bad that doesn't happen.

The second section of the level has a more orthodox structure than the first section. In the first section of the level, the player had to face a series of tracked saws that were much more difficult than they looked. The cognitive dissonance in that is very frustrating. The reverse happens in the second section, though: the level looks harder than it is. There is only one really taxing challenge, which is this pit full of saws.

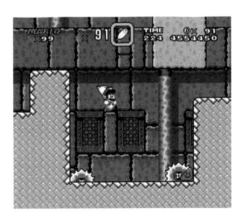

Because of the long descent, it can be difficult to nail the timing on this jump and land without taking damage. The effective landing area is reduced because Mario needs to land with room to run, so as to take advantage of the wall-running bumper corner. This is one of the only truly challenging descents in a dry level; most of the game's hardest challenges are lateral or ascending.

Although the rest of the level is easier than that one jump, there are still some qualitatively unusual evolutions. The jump pictured below has an odd combination of elements. It's above a pit full of periodic enemies, it's got a low ceiling, and there's another enemy that runs from right to left to intercept Mario's jump.

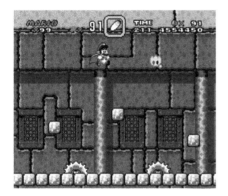 

Although this enemy comes at Mario like an intercept, the crucial skill here is still waiting. Trying to jump on the enemy (as one would do for an intercept) is not a good idea since it's invincible. Trying to jump over it would be very difficult because of the low ceiling. The player's best bet is to stop and let the Grinder pass before making the jump a moment later. This challenge gets back to the periodic enemies theme via an alternate route, but it still gets there.

The fireballs are not much of a threat either; much like we just saw at the end of the descending ceiling room in Ludwig's castle, these Fireballs are cued well in advance of Mario's jump. Most of the time, the Fireball will be descending by the time Mario needs to jump. If the player has the cape power-up, these jumps are quite easy. Even if the player doesn't have the cape, this section is only a trio of saws away from being a training-wheels challenge, even if it feels harder.

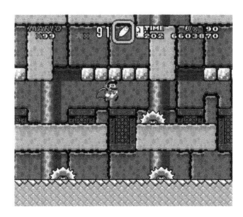

That said, these are not really indictments of this kind of level design. A level that seems harder than it really is can cause the player to experience the feeling of dominance and skillfulness. Videogames are often great because they can make players feel like their successes are much greater than they really are; this is a good example of the practice, achieved purely through design.

As a last note, I'd like to point out the massive optional challenge at the end of the level. With the cape, the player can fly over the game's widest lava pit, over more than a dozen fireballs, to a bonus door surrounded by 1-up mushrooms.

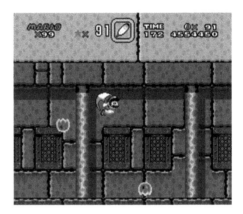

This kind of "feat of strength" challenge is a nice touch, when it's optional. It does show that at some point, the designers must have become aware of how game-breaking the ability for sustained flight could be.

Chocolate Fortress

Chocolate Fortress is made up of two complete cadences, the second of which is one of the clearest and most orderly cadences in the game. Both cadences in this level are in the periodic enemies theme. Why did the designers make a level of two distinct cadences, and what does that mean? The general idea is that the designers took a periodic enemy (the sharpened log) and iterated challenges that involve it until they reached the limits of what they thought was fun. Finding that their level wasn't long enough at that point, they chose a second idea and iterated it in a similar way. Thus, the level is divided into two clear sections that each take one idea and push its permutations as far as the designers thought it could go. The reason this succeeds, however, is that the designers are very strategic in how they iterate and for how long.

The first idea at work in the level is the pointed stick obstacle, which is introduced immediately. They work in more than one way, either in a pincer motion or moving in parallel. This is the standard challenge.

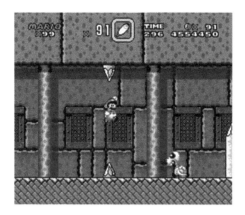

Immediately, the level commences with a series of evolutions. As you can see on the right, Mario must now make an ascending jump into a narrow aperture to get through the trap. The next jump adds an instant-death pit and a patrolling enemy on a small platform. (There was a patrolling enemy in the standard challenge, but he was easily avoided; not so in this case.) Every challenge after that includes some amount of these fireballs, which can spawn at any height every few seconds.

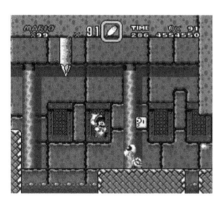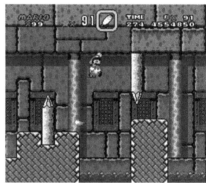

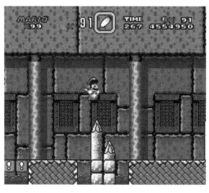

These fireballs represent the last evolution the level can bear before the designers felt like they needed a new standard challenge. This level has been about adding evolution after evolution, and it has been successful, but there is a limit to the number of new elements that can overlay the standard before a level starts to feel annoying rather than fun. When a level reaches that point, it's time for it to do something different.

In the second half of the level, the designers instituted a new standard challenge: the overhead Thwomp. You can see how the evolutions and expansions take place.

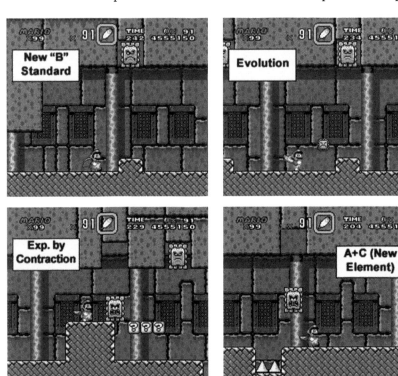

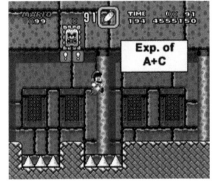

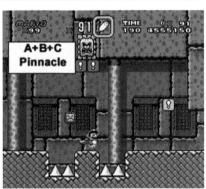

I've left a few of the challenges out of that image array to give a clearer picture of the primary thread of the evolutions. (That said, every challenge in this section does fit into the cadence in a logical way.) What we see here are three elements: the Thwomp of the standard challenge, a Thwimp that marks the first A+B evolution, and a pitfall that gives us a different "A+C" evolution. Using just these three elements, the designers create several iterations that play differently. As elegant as that is, the best thing about this level is that it finishes in one challenge that unites all three elements into a climactic A+B+C evolution. Not every level can do this; sometimes there are too many design ideas or mechanics in a level for the designers to put all of them in one challenge. Indeed, if the second half of this level had tried to incorporate the sharpened logs of the first half, it would have run into that problem. Because it drops that element to start over, it gains an elegant finale in return.

Wendy's Castle

Like Chocolate Fortress, Wendy's Castle breaks down into two sections. Although both levels are always in the periodic enemies theme, the two sections of Wendy's Castle are a little closer to one another in terms of game design ideas, and we'll see how. The basic idea behind the first section of Wendy's Castle is that it takes the sharpened logs of Chocolate Fortress and combines them with the deadly saws of Forest Fortress, but there are also some important differences. The sharpened logs have evolved into the giant smashing pillars pictured below. The behavior of the object is mostly the same—it's still a periodically-stabbing stick—but the size and speed of the attacks have both gone up, and now the entire object causes damage. Forest Fortress did something similar when it evolved the Urchin into the saw enemy, and then combined it with the overhead smasher.

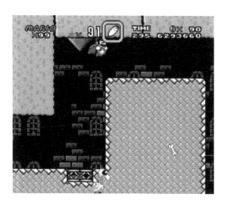 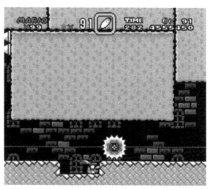

Why the first challenge must involve a springboard jump I cannot say for certain. It may be that the designers wanted to show that the giant smashing pillars will always cover the entire screen when extended; that's valuable data. I'm not sure a regular jump in an empty room wouldn't have served the same purpose. That said, springboards are fun once in a while, and this one doesn't detract from the level in any way. Immediately after this, the level throws a couple of tracked saws at Mario, but you can see how easy they are. This is just a warm-up.

The next challenge performs the obvious evolution, combining the saws with the smashing pillars. This time around, the level designers change the order of the evolutions so that the vertical saws come first (as they ought to), and the horizontally-tracked saws come second.

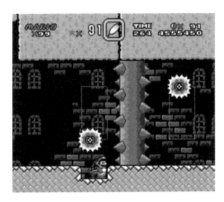

For challenges two and three, the designer's technique couldn't be clearer. It's a simple expansion: the number of saws goes up and the space between smashing spike pillars goes down. Even though all three of these challenges are geographically very close together, the pacing still works well because the player has to move through these challenges relatively slowly.

The next challenge takes away the smashing pillars and adds a series of platform jumps. The number of saws expands to three in a single challenge.

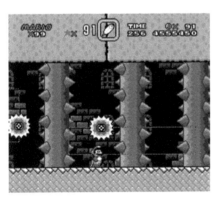
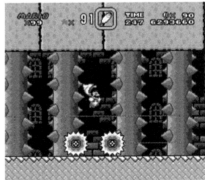

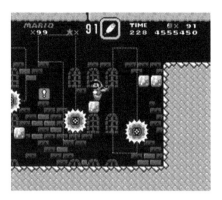

Additionally, if we think of the "safe spots" between the smashers in previous challenges as landing points, this challenge is an expansion upon that dimension, too. Each safe spot was at least two blocks wide, but each platform here is only one block wide. That's a classic expansion-by-contraction.

The second part of the level is different in substance, although very similar in structure. It's also a good example of how a series of expansion challenges ought to be done. For a final twist, this section also does something rare: it declines toward the moving targets theme. The reverse happens all the time; tons of moving targets levels cross into periodic enemy territory. It's much less common for moving platforms to show up in a level in any significant quantity outside their own theme, but they do appear here.

As in Chocolate Fortress, this level starts over with a new cadence at the halfway point. Despite the moving platforms, this section is still firmly in the periodic enemies theme, as almost every surface is guarded by a periodic enemy. After establishing a new standard challenge, the level develops a variety of different evolution and expansion challenges.

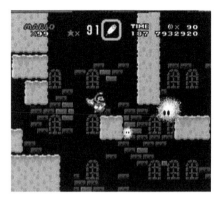 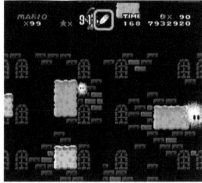

The most important thing about the expansion elements is that they're all different from one another. One-dimensional expansions (e.g., a pit jump getting wider and wider) are boring when placed in sequence, but *Super Mario World* rarely does something like that. In this section, the expanded element alternates: first the number of Hotheads expands, then number of platforms increases in an unhelpful way.

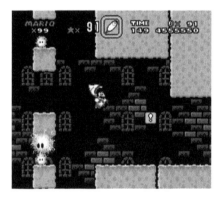

The last features three enemies orbiting three platforms. Rather than simply increase every element in every iteration, the designers expand the number of enemies, and then the number of platforms, back and forth. Finally, both elements reach their numerical peak in the level's last challenge.

Valley of Bowser 2 (Middle Section)

For the first part of Valley of Bowser 2, see the intercepts theme; that part of the level makes for an interesting point of comparison between the preservation of momentum and intercepts themes. This part of the level is an example of the periodic enemies theme, however, and one that deserves attention because of how badly executed it is.

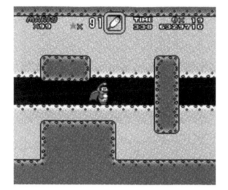
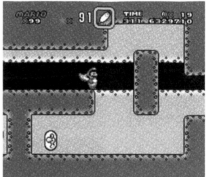

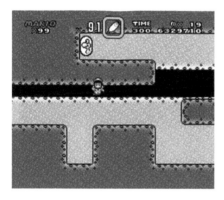

The idea behind this part of the level is clever: what if the level itself could be the periodic enemy? What if the path could be the obstacle? It certainly has most of the qualities of a periodic enemy: it is invincible, and it has a clearly timed behavior that it follows. Most importantly, it involves lots of waiting and walking and it diminishes the value of jumping. The problem is that it does this to such an extreme degree that it's hardly any fun. If Mario gets trapped between the moving pathway and a wall, he will die instantly, so the penalty is two at all times—a rare thing in this theme. This wouldn't be too bad, considering that this is one of the final levels, but there are some blind pathways that are completely inappropriate in this context, which you can see below.

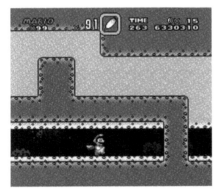
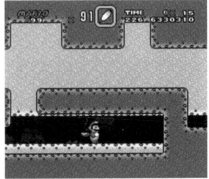
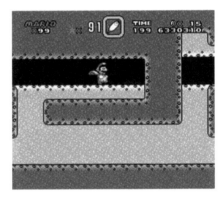

These pathways extend off-screen in such a way that if the player attempts them at the wrong time, Mario will be hopelessly trapped. The problem is that the player cannot know these runs are impossible the first time through—Mario has to die in order figure this out. Inescapable deaths are almost always a bad idea. I have written about this elsewhere, but many game designers report that one of their most useful metrics for playtesting is the question "whose fault was this death?" If the players consistently feel that it wasn't their fault, or that the difficulty was "cheap," then designers will often change a challenge's content. Miyamoto, Tezuka, and their team are normally virtuosic in their ability to avoid these kinds of deaths; players may lose lives while playing a level, but not because they found themselves in inescapable traps. This level and its blind alleys seems a little bit strange.

This section could have been remedied in a couple of ways that seem obvious. (Admittedly, I say this with the advantage of 25 years of hindsight, but lessons are lessons.) The first way was to simply remove these dead ends or give some greater reward for getting in and out so that the player isn't dying for absolutely nothing. These sections are so drudgingly slow that having to replay them is un-fun, when fun was supposed to be the goal. Another remedy would have been to simply break this corridor up into two or three sections. It depends how you count them, but there are at least six separate runs and four long periods of waiting in this section—without any break. It would have been easy to divide this in half and have a crossover challenge or something to break up the monotony in the middle. Monotony and frustration may have a place in the grand scheme of game design, but not in this game.

Soda Lake

Soda Lake is a clever and well-organized level, but one that introduces an unusual (and often frustrating) enemy: the Torpedo Ted. In the introduction, I noted that it's rare for an enemy to occupy a space not perfectly divisible into coin-block sizes. There are enemies who move through spaces that are not on a perfect block-sized grid, but not really any that travel in straight lines while occupying a non-integer amount of space. The Torpedo Ted's sprite does cut across these non-integer spaces. Additionally, most of the enemies in the game have either an accurate hitbox, or one that's generous to the player. The Torpedo Ted has a deceptive and unforgiving hitbox, especially on the front and back ends. Mario can easily take damage while apparently not touching him. The final problem is that the Torpedo Ted doesn't travel at a uniform speed, unlike almost every other enemy in the game. Instead, the Torpedo Ted accelerates smoothly after being released from its launcher. Despite all these problems, the level still develops in such an organized a way that the player can adjust to the increasing number of Torpedo Teds on screen.

As far as the level design goes, this level is neatly organized around a string of four expansions. The standard challenge for the level is easy to identify; it consists of single launcher in the middle of the screen. This challenge also shows us why this level is in the periodic enemies theme. Although the Torpedo Ted also looks a lot like an intercept, it's definitely a periodic enemy. Once the launcher starts firing torpedoes, it continues to do so in a regular fashion.

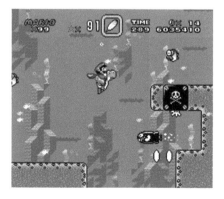 

Just as in earlier levels in this theme, the essential skill is moving past the periodic enemy when there are gaps in its attack pattern. That skill remains central throughout the level because of how clean and elegant the level design is. Almost all of the levels challenges are made up of nothing more than launchers in greater quantity and new configurations. For example, the second challenge is a simple expansion to two launchers.

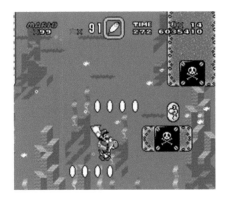 

The challenge after that (also pictured above) is simply an evolution in position that moves the launchers to the middle of the screen, where they're harder to get around. After that, there are two more expansions.

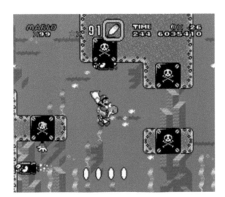 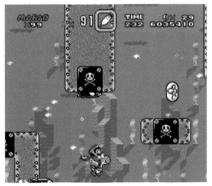

The expansions stop at four launchers. Realistically, there isn't room on the screen for five or six launchers, but that's not the only reason why the designers haven't added more. As I've stated before, consecutive expansions of the same type get boring and frustrating. Moreover, most Mario levels aren't that difficult, and they're not supposed to be. Thus, after peaking at four launchers, the level uses an evolution to restructure them for the next challenge.

Then, the last challenge reduces the number of launchers, but performs a significant expansion-by-contraction on the available space for Mario to swim through by putting a floor underneath the three launchers. This way, the designers are able to squeeze in one more expansion, by expanding a different aspect of the standard challenge.

Valley Fortress

Valley Fortress represents the culmination of the periodic enemies theme and offers us a great lesson in difficulty which is both organized and fair. It also shows us that levels don't have to employ radical design strategies in order to be great.

This is the standard challenge (left); it reintroduces the smashing spiked pylon in a context that is otherwise penalty-free. One unusual feature here is the stair-like descent of the platforms during this standard challenge. The purpose of this, if it was intentional, is to help establish a frame of reference for the player for how much distance Mario can cross during one cycle of the pylons. The length (in blocks) of each platform is obvious because of the way they're staggered.

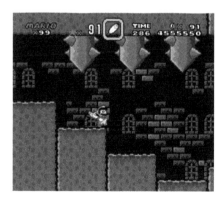 

After the standard challenge, the level bounces over from periodic enemies to a kind of non-thematic action section. The first few enemies will later be integrated into the cadence of this level, but not in the way they appear here.

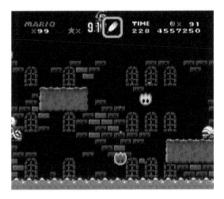

These fireballs, on the other hand, are in a totally normal, periodic enemies design. These will later be the "B" element that gets added to the level's pinnacle challenge via an evolution.

The first proper evolution and evolution/expansion of the standard challenge contain obvious changes. The solid, safe gaps between the smashing spike pylons disappear and are replaced by spike pits. (Note that this is an evolution because some new element is introduced. The penalty for the standard challenge was already one, and that has not changed yet.)

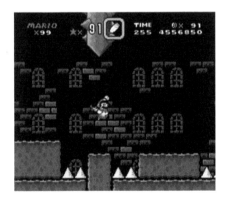 

This evolution reduces number of pylons from the standard (which had sets of three pylons in a row) but evolves the challenge by adding two spike pits. This evolution is then succeeded by a challenge that expands the d-distance.

The next challenge expands the number of pylons, while maintaining the form of the first evolution (below, left). After that, the next challenge bounces back to the periodic fireballs introduced before. This time, those fireball pit-jumps are evolved via the addition of enemies on the platforms (below, right).

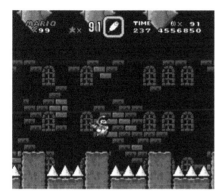 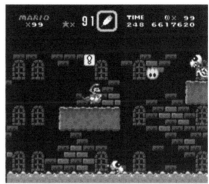

At this point, the level has introduced all of its various elements, and now only has to combine them.

Although it consists of only cadence, this level divides neatly in two. The dividing point comes in the next evolution/expansion, during which the smashing pylons start moving at twice their previous speed. The first challenge in this new section drops the number of pylons down to one so that the player can get accustomed to the new speed with an easier challenge. That said, this expansion also increases the penalty to two by exchanging spike pits for lava pits and adds a fireball to a pylon challenge for the first time.

 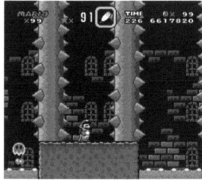

The next island expands the previous challenge by adding an additional pylon, but it also drops the fireball. Then, this challenge evolves and expands into the pinnacle challenge by bringing the fireball back and changing the d-distance.

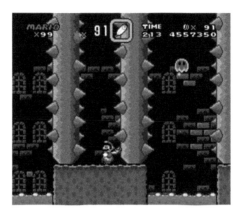

The pinnacle challenge also has a shorter platform, but that's not part of the expansion because its effect is entirely psychological. As far as Mario's momentum is concerned, there's no difference between a three-block platform and a five-block platform. Psychologically, it feels more intimidating, but the contraction of the platform has no material effect on the jump. The part of this jump that *is* an expansion is the extra danger added by getting past the pylon on the opposite side. Mario can't simply land on the edge of the next platform and stay there; he has to keep going into the middle of the next platform before he can wait safely. This jump looks as though it has a d-distance of five, when really it has a d-distance of seven.

The last jump in the cadence brings the level of difficulty down, considerably. This challenge would most accurately be termed an evolution of the first challenge in the second half of the level. This time, one of the smashing pylons stabs upwards.

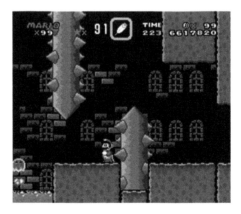

This challenge is easy because the d-distance is only two. Why include it then? I think that this challenge is supposed to serve as a denouement for the level. The designers knew how, relative to the rest of the game, this level is very difficult.

The last jump, especially, requires the greatest level of precision of any in the skill theme. This simpler challenge brings down the level of tension and allows the player to spend a moment appreciating what he or she has just accomplished before moving onto the mid-boss fight.

Looking back at the level, the most impressive thing about it is how elegant the cadence is. There are really only three core design ideas: smashing pylons, pitfalls, and fireballs. Using only those elements, speeding them up, and changing the size of platforms, the designers are able to craft a challenging (but engaging) cadence. Many of the young designers I have encountered try to constantly surprise the player by introducing one-off mechanics, unexpected twists and extreme expansions of normal design ideas. Sometimes, that can work. I think that this level proves surprises and extremes aren't necessary for a great level. Tubular (which we'll examine later) is surprising, inventive, exotic, and horrible. Valley Fortress is formulaic, but still very enjoyable. The lesson, to distill it to its essence, is that if you have good mechanics and a good organizational system for implementing them, you don't need anything more.

6

The Preservation of Momentum Theme

The preservation of momentum skill theme is all about sending Mario through challenges that require a quick exit at full momentum, and then slowly making that exit more and more difficult. The stats on this theme are what one would expect. This theme features the biggest average d-distance and the largest delta height. Because Mario needs to keep up his momentum to get through challenges quickly, that same momentum is going to make it easier for him to gain height and distance on his jumps. Moreover, this means that if the player doesn't keep up Mario's momentum, it will greatly endanger him. There's a negative feedback loop embedded in that dynamic. Once Mario loses his momentum, it can take a relatively large amount of time and effort to get it back. Thus, the player can sometimes find him or herself in a scenario where the subjective difficulty shoots up all of a sudden.

Like its complement on the platforming side of the composite, the preservation of momentum theme is heavy on iteration and light on accumulation. Only two levels really build up traditional accumulations: Forest of Illusion 4 and Awesome. (That said, Awesome *really* goes crazy with accumulations). The iterations in this theme are a lot more appreciable for the player than they are in the moving targets theme because of how different they all look and feel. The mechanics of momentum don't change that much. Instead, the difference in the feel of levels comes from the feedback that drives the player: there's always some new reason to keep moving at full momentum. The theme begins this with sinking platforms in Yoshi's Island 4.

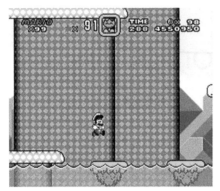

Although they're hardly any danger, the sinking of these platforms will keep the player moving forward. Skipping ahead, a similar thing occurs in Star World 5, which features a long gauntlet of falling platforms. These two levels are not close to each other chronologically, but it's interesting that they are two out of only three levels in the game to make use of the traditional sinking/falling platform in a fully developed cadence. Falling or sinking platforms were a staple of *Super Mario Bros*, and *Super Mario Bros. 3*. For some reason, they're rare in *Super Mario World*.

That reason might just be that the designers didn't need them because they had no problem implementing other reasons for Mario to keep running. In Donut Plains 4, the player faces rising pipes and lots of overhead intercept enemies.

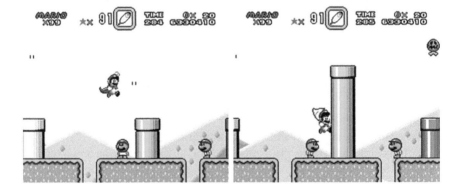

This level is actually the first to introduce overhead intercepts, and it does so outside the intercepts theme. (This is the only time that happens). Both the extending pipes and Hammer Brothers give Mario excellent reasons to keep going at full momentum. The former requires momentum to gain the proper height and leap over the full extension of the pipe, and the latter involves a relatively dangerous enemy whose death is unnecessary, grants no reward, and is just as easily bypassed as fought. Third, the player faces both of those things beneath an endless rain of enemies in the second half of the level, and it becomes very clear to the player that it's best to run rather than fight.

Eventually, high jumps and endless enemies come together in the first real accumulation of the theme. Forest of Illusion 4 uses the extending pipe, but this time also throws in the hovering Lakitu who will rain down Spikey enemies constantly. Lakitus dwelling in the pipes do this too.

The Spikey enemy isn't invincible, but it is harder to kill than a normal enemy. The Lakitus also won't stop throwing them until the screen is nearly covered with them. Thus, it's better for Mario to just flee. The high and/or extending pipes and Lakitus just make jumping with momentum a greater necessity. Some of this carries over into Chocolate Secret and Valley of Bowser 4, which both feature projectile-launching Chucks.

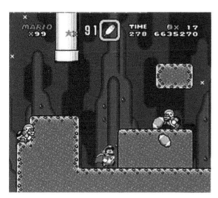 

Although the Chucks launch projectiles in a regular fashion, this is not a periodic enemy. Firstly, in both scenarios, Mario has to jump because of the terrain and the projectiles act like intercepts for those jumps. Secondly, short and well-timed runs will not help Mario much here. He needs speed to get past the Chuck and to get enough height on his jumps to get over the projectiles if they come close to him. Good timing doesn't hurt, but that skill alone won't get him through these challenges.

We'll see lots of examples of how this theme requires Mario to keep up his momentum, but makes it increasingly difficult to do so. Some levels, however, turn that idea on its head. In icy levels, Mario's momentum is conserved by the slippery surfaces of the level itself. This idea first appears in Donut Secret 2, but the best example of this is the pinnacle of the theme.

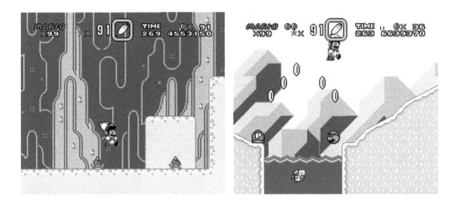

Many of the challenges in this level look like they would be rather easy except for the icy terrain that makes control of Mario's momentum more difficult. This highlights the core skill of the theme; it isn't about merely rushing headlong into every situation, it's about controlling Mario's momentum and reacting quickly to sudden changes appear. Awesome really hammers this home.

The combination is tough—not only does the player have to deal with a large number of enemies that can totally surround Mario if he stands still for even a second, but the player has to do on small icy platforms. In other words, the player really needs to be able to think ahead and react quickly because small miscalculations can become fatal very quickly.

Yoshi's Island 4

Like most of the skill themes, the preservation of momentum theme begins with a training-wheels challenge. Unlike the other themes that do this, though, the preservation of momentum theme has a problem: it has to convince the player to keep Mario moving. To force the player's hand, an element of danger has to be introduced. This challenge does a good job of accomplishing everything in one go.

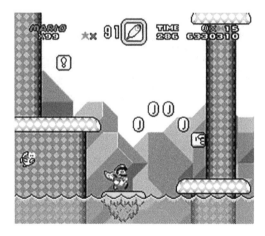

These platforms slowly sink into the water as Mario stands on them. The player will, eventually, react to this by jumping off the platform and onto dry land. The incentive to jump off the platform quickly and keep Mario's momentum moving forward is obvious. Yet, the danger of the challenge is mostly negated because of the water below the platform. Even if the player waits and sinks, Mario won't lose a life immediately. Thus, these challenges work perfectly to show the player the value of preserving Mario's forward momentum and preserve an inexperienced player's small stockpile of lives with an unconventional set of training-wheels.

The second challenge is the standard challenge for the level: two sinking platforms in sequence. While swimming in the water is possible, it's slow and boring. Jumping on both of these platforms is fun, but the player needs to be quick about it, even if failing isn't fatal. It evolves in the next challenge.

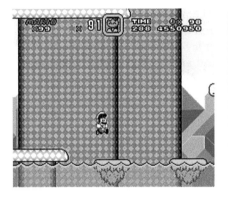 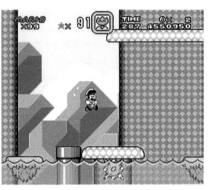

Here, you can see the first proper intercepts of the level, but it's important to recognize that one of those intercepts is actually not a danger at all. The left spike ball floats harmlessly under the dry-land platform, serving as a good warning shot that alerts the player that the next intercepts are coming.

After this, there is a short punctuating challenge with a puzzle element. The player must activate the P-Bridge and then shoot the shell across it. The player does have to be quick here, but this challenge doesn't belong to the preservation of momentum theme in any conventional way. After the bridge, the level continues iterating the standard challenge. The number of intercepts expands from one to two.

 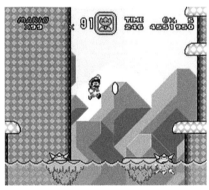

After that, there are three platforms and three intercepts in yet another obvious expansion. Importantly, the d-distances between these platforms have not increased. Three identical jumps of this kind are not mechanically more difficult than two identical jumps, but to a new player it can be psychologically more taxing. This is yet another example of positive deception on the behalf of the designers—something we will see a lot in this theme.

Finally, there is a mutation challenge that illustrates one of the aspects of mutations that bears considerable study. This leaping fish stands in for the spiky intercepts of the previous challenges. It is different in appearance and behavior than the obstacle it replaces, but the kind of difference is important.

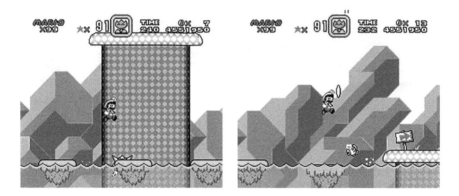

The jump this fish forces Mario to take is only slightly different. It's a little higher and a little narrower as well. Momentum-wise, there's no change. In essence, this jump is calibrated so that it's no more difficult than the previous challenge, just different. That's a perfect example of a mutation. What the mutation jump does best is to show the player another use for a skill he or she already has, without asking anything new of him or her. The way this jump controls for angle while maintaining virtually every other variable is a great example of how mutations are done, when they're done well.

Donut Secret 2

As I noted in Chapter 2, *Super Mario World* gets rid of the turn-and-slide mechanic present in *Super Mario Bros.* and *Super Mario Bros. 3*. When Mario reverses course in *SMW*, no matter how strong his momentum is, he will go in the new direction instantly as long as he is on normal ground. This level does away with the new stop-on-a-dime mechanics and goes toward the other extreme. Everything is covered in ice, creating a low-friction surface that makes it much harder to reverse course quickly. Mario veterans will resort to the momentum-breaking back-jump that was so essential in earlier titles. New players will be learning how to do that jump, along with a few other skills in this level. Essentially, what this level is out to do is force the player to use momentum-controlling (rather than momentum-halting) skills by taking away Mario's ability to stop.

Often, levels that undermine one of a game's fundamental mechanics (like being able to stop) can be terribly mean-spirited and generally disliked. It doesn't make sense to teach your players to expect something and then take it away for spite. Donut Secret 2 gets away with it because of how well-placed all the level's challenges are. Players can't halt Mario's momentum, but they don't need to.

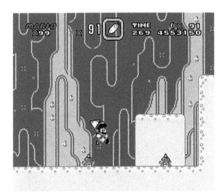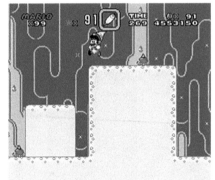

The spaces where Mario is supposed to land and then jump again are obvious. The key is that not only does Mario have to jump in the right places, but he needs to work with the icy momentum to get to the top of the high cliff and avoid the enemies. Combat is possible with the cape, but that will send Mario into a wall, breaking his momentum and causing him to have to start back along the slippery terrain, away from his destination.

One thing that will help in almost all the jumps is a cape glide, which can give an airborne Mario the few moments the player needs to plan out the next few actions. Cape glides also help to preserve momentum for later use.

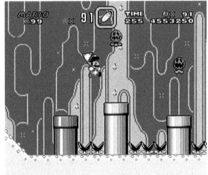

With the nearly inevitable momentum from the downhill, these two Leaping Pumpkin Plants lie in Mario's most convenient jump-paths. At less than maximum height, however, a cape glide will cut across the pipes nicely. All the player has to do is break out of the slide without going to full height—or by peaking before the first Pumpkin and dropping beneath them with a glide.

There are only two other real challenges in the main part of this level, and they're both evolutions on the original idea. You can see on the left here how the empty platforms are now occupied by enemies.

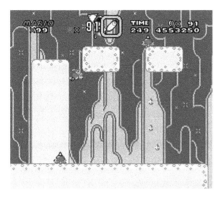 

That's a fairly standard evolution, adding an enemy that forces an earlier, more controlled jump. There's also a small expansion-by-contraction, as these platforms are smaller than in the earlier platforms in the level. The challenge above and right, on the other hand, does something more interesting. Here we see a long line of enemies that necessitate good momentum for a long jump. The tricky part is getting over the whole group and still being able to catch the edge of the cliff and ascend. (Bouncing off one of the Koopas would also help, but that too is an exercise in preserving and controlling momentum). This is another good time for a cape glide, and it teaches a very important, but subtle, lesson: cape glides do not always need to continue all the way to the ground. Aborting a cape-glide in mid-flight is an important skill, and this is probably the first instance where that skill is emphasized, so that Mario doesn't glide right off the cliff edge.

There's a pipe section in this level, accessible from around the mid-point, that sticks with the skill theme but uses a totally different mechanic. These platforms will drop from under Mario after a second or two, necessitating a quick jump and continued momentum, and are nicely interrupted by a couple of Leaping Pumpkin Plants. Alternatively, Mario can use the P-balloon powerup.

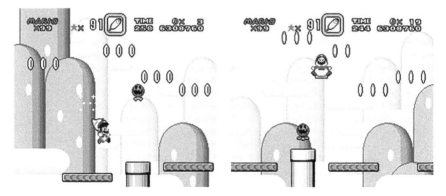

I will go on record expressing my distaste for the balloon powerup, and use this opportunity to explain some of that distaste. What does the balloon add here that jumping on the platforms doesn't do more elegantly? The distribution of the coins suggests that this section is supposed to teach the player how to control Mario while he is under the effects of the balloon powerup. Perhaps it works a very cursory introduction to that. The cape powerup is fast, nuanced, and intuitive; this balloon section is slow, tedious, and unhelpful. If the balloon were taken out, this section would still make sense with the rest of the level, and indeed would be a nice contrast, showing how the icy floors and falling platforms are two aspects of the same thematic idea, connecting them in the player's mind.

The final challenge is a hallmark of Miyamoto games: the reward-by-fun. Here we see a stack of that which are easily dispatched by one jump.

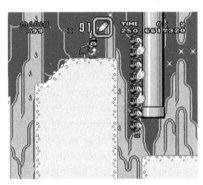

The designers do this several times in the game: giving the player an easy-but-flashy challenge that lets them feel dominant as a reward for completing harder sections. Not all feedback mechanisms need to be items, secrets, or cutscenes. Easy, flashy, and fun challenges are good rewards as well.

Donut Plains 4

Donut Plains 4 offers a series of challenges that are clearly in the preservation of momentum theme, but only the first half of the level has anything resembling normal cadence development, while the second part of the level is less organized. The standard challenge is this:

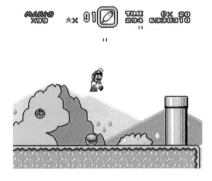

This challenge involves leaping to a higher platform to avoid an enemy that is better avoided than engaged, the rainbow-shell Koopa. It is possible to defeat this enemy before it becomes dangerous by running at a full clip and jumping on the Koopa before he gets into the shell. Without that foresight, the irregular movements and resistance to jump damage mean it's simpler to leap over the enemy with a momentum jump or cape glide (or both). The point of this enemy is to train the player to make the jump quickly and in full stride. The rest of the requires a similar strategy, although often in a very different context.

This next challenge is a simple expansion and evolution of the first challenge. There are two enemies on the ground and one enemy that leaps out of the far-side pipe. The challenge after that is a little more interesting.

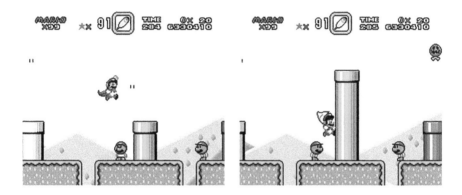

In this challenge, there's just one standard Koopa. Technically, there's a chance of dying in the pitfall in the middle, but it's not very likely. The real threat of this challenge is that the player will miss the jump when the pipe on the far side extends upwards by several blocks. In the end, the delta height changes by four in just over a second's time. Just like the rainbow shell enemy, the point of this extending pipe is to teach the player to keep Mario's momentum up to take bigger jump. This one doesn't require full momentum, but a simple standing jump will result in Mario falling into the path of the Koopa below.

Just after the first extending pipe challenge, the leaping Pumpkin Plant from the previous challenge is added to the existing setup in a simple evolution, giving the player another reason to jump with as much momentum as possible. After that, there is a Flyin' Hammer Brother that Mario can run past. In fact, the design suggests he should run past it at full momentum without engaging because of the wall-ramp on the other side.

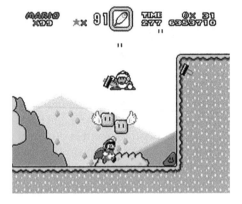

It's definitely possible to defeat a Hammer Brother, but there's not always a reason to do so. In this case, it's clear the designers meant Mario to simply run on. This idea repeats in a different form a couple of challenges later. Here, if Mario descends the blue pipe, he'll be shot out the next pipe at an angle.

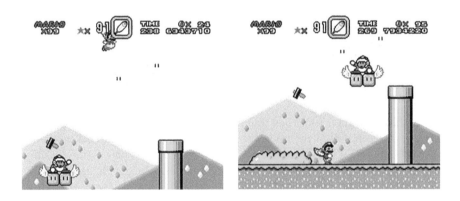

As long as the player doesn't do anything to interrupt Mario's momentum, Mario will land on the far side of the pipe, and avoid the Hammer Brother entirely. Otherwise, Mario either has to run backwards to get enough momentum to make a flying leap or has to defeat Hammer Brother and use his platform to get out.

The next challenge within the cadence gives Mario the chance at collecting the star powerup. Almost every instance of a star powerup happens in the preservation of momentum theme. It makes the most sense for Mario to cover as much ground as possible while invincible. As is common in this theme, there are momentum-breaking obstacles placed in his way. This pit-jump is actually one of the game's largest in terms of combined d-distance and delta height.

The small hills that come afterwards also slow Mario down a bit, but not enough to break his momentum entirely. Should Mario stop and/or lose the effect of the star, however, the enemies will rain down endlessly, making this section much more difficult. The final jump in the level is a simple expansion of the first jump with the star.

The size and shape of the jump are similar, and the Hammer Brother is present as well, but the penalty has gone up from one to two. Mario could wait, kill the Hammer Brother, and use his platform, but a jump at full momentum will also carry him across the gap and into the end-goal.

Forest of Illusion 4

Forest of Illusion 4 is an inter-level evolution upon Donut Plains 4, focusing on situations where it behooves Mario to get past enemies as fast as possible. This level includes two features that up the ante over the previous level. The first and most obvious is the ever-present cloud Lakitu, who will start throwing down

Spiny enemies when Mario grabs the dangling 1-up—even if by accident. He is an evolution upon the Flyin' Hammer Brother, who was limited to one location. The other evolution is the Lakitu residing in a pipe, who will similarly hurl out Spiny after Spiny once Mario is in his aggro radius. This enemy likes to pop out of the pipe when throwing, effectively adding one block of height to the pipe itself. Both these enemies require swift action, or else the number of Spiny enemies can quickly grow to the point that Mario is faced with an insoluble mess. On the right, below, you can see the standard challenge for the level, a Lakitu in a short pipe.

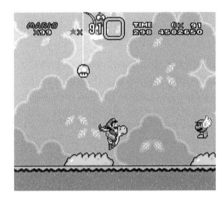
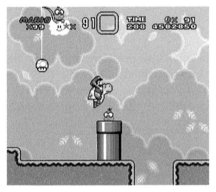

This Lakitu is an evolution of the extending pipes found in Donut Plains 4; the Lakitu's head acts as a further extension of the pipe, in addition to throwing enemies. The pipe Lakitu immediately expands (pictured below, left), increasing the height of the pipe to the point that Mario needs real momentum to get above the Lakitu's head, which can be as high as seven blocks in its full extended position. The problem is that this momentum jump will probably collide with the 1-up, beginning the Spiny rain.

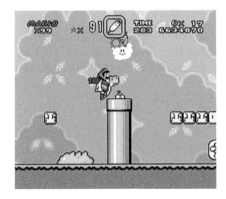

6. The Preservation of Momentum Theme

After that expansion comes an evolution/expansion (pictured above, middle), which is just slightly taller than the standard challenge, but adds the coin-block ceiling to the left. The ceiling stops lower, long-range jumps and can also trap slower players in a confined space with an increasing number of Spinies. It doesn't do either of those things particularly well, but it's possible. The last real iteration of this (below) evolves the challenge by putting the pitfall in front of the Lakitu, causing the player to jump both in one go.

 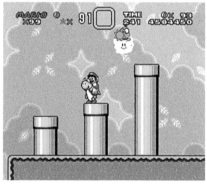

The extending pipe returns in the second half of the level, serving the same role as it did in Donut Plains 4. This time, however, the hovering Lakitu in a cloud can collide with Mario as he leaps over the tall pipes. Thus, not only does the player need to keep Mario's momentum up to make higher jumps, but he or she also needs to stay at full speed to get over the extending pipe before it reaches its max height. This challenge itself evolves into the right image above. Here, the challenge of the extending pipe is magnified. The player still needs to keep Mario's momentum up because the Lakitu can and will drop Spinies on the pipes, giving Mario no room and no time to deal with them. They'll also fall into the gaps between the pipes, taking away those spaces as landing areas.

The cadence ends with a pinnacle challenge that nearly fills the screen with enemies. The variety of enemies is surprising; the only threat until this point has been the Lakitu and his Spiny spawns. What all of these enemies have in common, though, is that they're not susceptible to an easy jump.

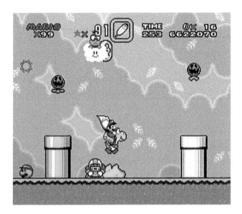

The Chuck, Pumpkins, and dropped Spiny enemies are all set up in such a way that a combat jump isn't going to solve problems. Instead, it's better to simply get in and out of this space between the pipes as soon as possible. The sudden appearance of a variety of enemies is a major evolutionary shift away from what has come before in this level, but it's still appropriate for the cadence and theme.

Chocolate Island 2

Chocolate Island 2 is built around a variable midsection, a section that is the only real point of interest from a design perspective. The essential idea behind the level is that the second section will change based on whether Mario has collected a certain number of coins or has a certain amount of time on the clock. The specific number of coins or seconds doesn't matter for our study; there's no lasting lesson to be learned from the specific number. The overall premise—that the content of the level changes based on how the player plays it—is interesting as a concept too, but that's not a lesson in itself. It would be easy for a young designer, attempting a similar level, to make a level with dynamic sections that feels completely incoherent. Chocolate Island 2 coheres because it stays within the preservation of momentum theme no matter which middle section the player encounters. It does not, however, feature a fully developed cadence because those sections could come in any order. Nevertheless, there are some interesting evolutions.

The section commonly referred to as "A" is the only section in the game that requires a soaring cape jump to reach the end of a level. While there have been many sections that suggest or even reward flight with the cape, none have forced the issue. Moreover, not since Donut Plains 1 has any section of a level rewarded the player with a secret path for sustaining Mario's horizontal momentum through the air. Section A of Chocolate Island 2 does both of these things, and in the greater context of the game this makes sense. The ability to sustain Mario's flight with the cape indefinitely (via an "air bounce") was included in the game probably as a difficult skill that few people would master. Perhaps for a short amount of time around Christmas 1990, that was true. Since then, players all over the world have used sustained flight to break the heck out of the game. This is the one case in which sustained flight with the cape is actually necessary.

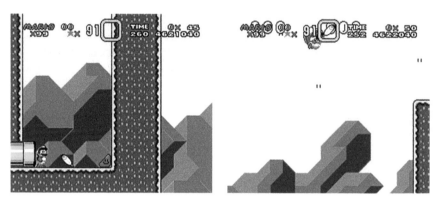

This involves preservation of momentum in two different ways. The running start is clearly in the preservation of momentum theme, but actually sustaining and controlling the flight is a preservation of momentum challenge as well. To emphasize the player's need for disciplined control over Mario's flying momentum, the coins are set into single lines that are only accessible to the tightest air-bounces. It's reminiscent of the similar section in Donut Plains 1, though it's odd because it comes so late in the game. Then again, we can't judge the designers for trying not to overexpose the technique which they must have known could break their game.

The middle section known traditionally as "B" is still a series of preservation of momentum-themed challenges, but it's impressive how different it is from the previous option. This section features sloping cliffs interrupted by variously pathed Wing Koopas. The effect of the cliffs is rather like that of the icy levels elsewhere in this theme; while on the slopes Mario's momentum is never comes to a rest. A few slopes later, the designers use an obvious but extremely effective evolution.

Once the slopes are directing Mario's momentum *toward* the enemies, the player is better off just bouncing off the Wing Koopas in sequence. In fact, the player could have gotten through most of this level by jumping on those enemies. That's where the next evolution comes in. There are two chains of Koopas, if we count the big gap in the middle to be the start of a new challenge. In each chain of Koopas, they all start their patrols within the same two blocks of height, and so bouncing from one to another is easy. The fifth Koopa in both sets, however, starts its flight about three blocks higher and is cued to begin the upward portion of his flight just a little bit earlier.

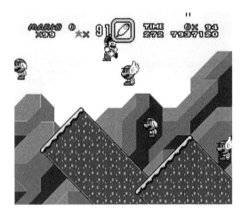

This means that players who have gotten in a groove bouncing from one Koopa to the next will be rudely interrupted by a Koopa who is suddenly too high. This effect is enhanced because the changes in Koopas heights and the changes the shape of the ramps below don't happen at the same times. This is a subtle incorporation of the intercepts side of the composite, which emphasizes fast reactions and adaptations rather than steady forward momentum.

The middle section usually referred to as "C" offers yet another very different iteration of a preservation of momentum series of challenges. This section brings back the Rex enemy not seen since the beginning of the game. These stacked cliffs are filled with Rexes that offer a clear but difficult jump-path for Mario.

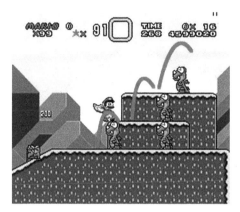

The reason these are Rexes and not Koopas is not just because Rexes are taller and make for more difficult jumps, but also because Rexes always walk off cliff edges (whereas Koopas can either walk off or turn around), forcing the player hurry and jump before a Rex walks off the cliff and blocks the way. There are a couple of fairly obvious but less likely alternatives: because of the Rex's tendency to walk off cliffs, Mario could simply wait. As it has been explained elsewhere, however, waiting more than a few seconds is boring and players aren't likely to do it. The other option is combat, and that would be a reasonably easy option, but even then the player still needs to hustle Mario up the slope to stay out of a situation in which the Rex is dropping down on Mario, which makes combat almost impossible. Mario has to be at the same height or higher than enemies he tries to fight, regardless of which powerup he uses to do that. But in two out of three of those cases, Mario's solutions are clearly in the preservation of momentum theme, like the rest of the level.

Star World 5

All Star Road levels tend toward some kind of design extreme, and Star World 5 exhibits many game design ideas that become obvious to an observer because of their extremity. To start, we see in this level one of the design features that has been mostly (and perhaps oddly) absent from *Super Mario World*: the falling platform. Comparatively speaking, there were a lot more of these in *Super Mario Bros. 3*, and the paucity of them in *Super Mario World* suggests that the designers were interested in moving on. Nevertheless, this particular level is filled with them, and long chains of them form two major sections.

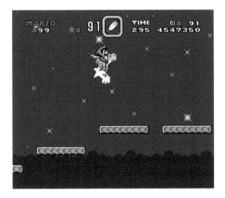 

What is also clear in these sections is the placement and behavior of momentum-assisting enemies. Notice how the Wing Koopas aren't in a position that makes jumping terribly difficult. Instead, they're configured so that it's easy for the player to bounce off them and glide over the falling platforms entirely.

There is also this rather extreme exercise pictured below, which involves the string of coins mechanic, and a P-switch that activates it. The reason I call this extreme is that it goes so far into the preservation of momentum theme that it becomes an abstraction of the idea. The player has to use the coins and p-block to build a runway for Mario that will take him over an enormous (>15 blocks) pitfall.

 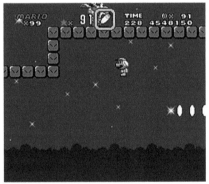

The player has to build this runway without seeing it. The screen does not scroll with the coin blocks, so the player has to just guess where to steer it. That lack of control is out of character for this game. That said, it is in the preservation of momentum theme. It's also in the Star Road, which is where the game is supposed to be experimental and weird.

Chocolate Secret

Although Awesome is definitely the pinnacle of the preservation of momentum theme, Chocolate Secret emphasizes one aspect of the theme more fully than any

6. The Preservation of Momentum Theme

other level: preservation of momentum by avoidance. The preservation of momentum theme rests in the platforming declension, and I've classified it that way because in these levels, action solutions to problems are less appropriate than platforming solutions. It would be a mistake to equate the presence of numerous enemies with a level being in the action declension, and this level shows us why. Levels rich in enemies are often action levels, but it's the *way* that the player deals with the enemies that really signifies the theme, not the quantity of enemies present. This level puts Mario into challenges where full momentum is necessary for two reasons. First, the Kicking Chuck's football is deadly and a large number of them can accumulate in a small space if Mario doesn't attack or bypass the Chuck quickly. Second, many of the Chucks sit at a high point in the terrain, meaning that Mario needs momentum to quickly the slopes and platforms between himself and the enemy.

The slopes and levels of the later challenges are the first element to be introduced. Most of the enemies in this level are either resistant to fireballs or completely immune to them. This is an obvious limit on action solutions to the problems presented, but in addition to that, the slopes present in this level make it much harder to use the cape or Yoshi's tongue to kill enemies. The image below isn't the standard challenge, it's more of a warning shot, but it does illustrate the problem of slopes in this level.

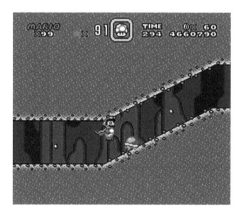

Because the Beetle is coming downwards at Mario, his attacks are more difficult to target, and this is doubly true with the very low ceiling. What the player really needs to do is quickly run up the hill into the part of the tunnel that has some headroom. This allows Mario to either jump over the enemy or jump on it. In either case, losing Mario's full momentum will result in having to face the Beetle on the hill, making it harder to avoid damage.

The next challenge is the standard from which the rest of the cadence is derived. The Kicking Chuck launches one of the game's only truly unpredictable projectiles. The football in question bounces at variable heights between two and six blocks, and when two of them are on screen at the same time, the challenge can get crowded. Because the Kicking Chucks never stop launching projectiles, and because they will turn to face Mario wherever he is, the easiest solution is just to run and jump past the Chuck so fast that he never gets a chance to kick a football.

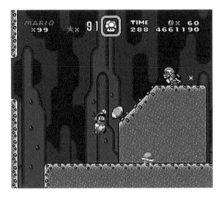 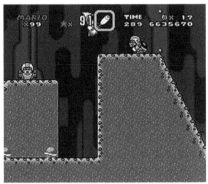

Unlike the Pitching Chuck, which starts firing as soon as Mario sees him, the Kicking Chuck has a built-in delay. That delay helps, but there's still the problem of climbing these slopes. It's easy enough to defeat the lower Chuck with a cape attack before the barrage of footballs begins, but that removes the easiest path. The simplest thing to do is charge the first Chuck, bounce off his head to keep Mario's momentum, and then use the height from that bounce to get over any other footballs and the remaining Chuck. In either case, the player isn't really engaging these Chucks in sustained combat, he or she is just rushing past them.

Following the standard, there is an evolution/expansion that increases the gradient of the hill and the distance Mario has to cover to get past the Chuck. It also features a pipe that backs the Chuck and narrows the aperture through which Mario can slip while maintaining momentum. The pipe is an evolution because it's a totally new element. The expansion here is in the distance Mario has to cover. From the bottom lip of the previous slope to the pinnacle of the current slope, Mario has to ascend eight blocks and travel twelve blocks laterally—four of which are pitfall d-distance.

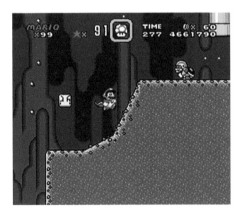

6. The Preservation of Momentum Theme

All the while, the Chuck can start kicking footballs if Mario isn't up the slope fast enough. For this reason, there's only one Chuck; two seems like it might have been too cruel.

The next challenge is actually an evolution of the first two-Chuck challenge. This time, the Chucks are in a walled space that allows the footballs to bounce around in every direction. Thankfully, the jumps and runs are much shorter and easier. By that same token, the terrain can be a real hazard if the player doesn't exit quickly through the pipe. The footballs can really accumulate.

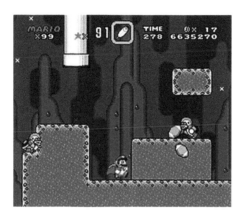

At full momentum, this challenge can be exceedingly brief. Losing momentum can trap Mario in a prison of bouncing footballs. This is one of the clearest examples in the game of how important momentum can be even in the absence of a large pitfall.

Next, there is a section whose intent is clear, but whose failure is the more obvious for that clarity. This set of giant, plunging slopes would make for a great reward-by-fun section if it were executed a little bit more carefully. Rewards-by-fun require a baseline level of ease punctuated by small, easy challenges and a rapid stream of rewards.

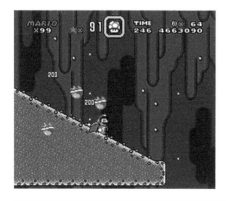 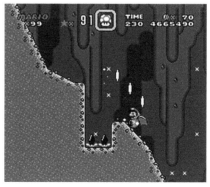

The basic idea here is that Mario can slide all the way to the bottom, knocking off Buzzy Beetles as he goes. It is easy, and it does fit in the skill theme. The problem is that there's nothing interesting at stake. Although Mario can slide almost the whole way down, sliding through consecutive enemies doesn't grant Mario a 1-up the way consecutive jumps or shell-kills do. Thus, the player has nothing to focus on to tie this area together.

The last section gives us two instances of the same idea: an evolution challenge featuring uneven terrain and lots of enemies who aren't easy to fight and require either swift action or all-out avoidance. The first part of this section shows us crenelated terrain swarming with dangerous, spiked enemies. Because they're small and invulnerable to jump and fireball attacks, these enemies are a pain to deal with, especially in large numbers.

Stopping to enter combat is a bad idea because there are enemies coming in both directions; it's better to maintain Mario's momentum and use the cape to make long, gliding jumps from high platform to high platform, avoiding the lower areas entirely. Later in the level, the challenge evolves by substituting the Chuck in for the spiked enemy. The Chucks don't do more damage than the previous enemy, but they will follow Mario, making them a little more dangerous. As before, Mario is better of running through this section because all six Chucks in this section can stack up on one screen, resulting in a much greater challenge.

In between the spiked enemies and the Chucks there is a totally different challenge that still maintains the same skill theme. Here the player has to quickly cross a sinking platform, while various obstacles stand between Mario and the other side.

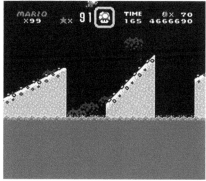

After the chucks, there second stretch of sinking platforms that evolves the first by changing the slope of the platforms the same way the designers did in Chocolate Island 2.

The Charging Chucks and sinking platforms don't constitute a second cadence to the level; both parts of the second half only evolve once. They do evolve in clever and unique ways, and are clearly related to the skill theme of the level.

Valley of Bowser 4

Valley of Bowser 4 introduces the Digging Chuck, and uses his unique projectile in a large number of innovative ways. The boulder that this Chuck launches behaves different than those launched by Chucks and other enemies because it depends on the terrain more meaningfully than any of the other launched intercepts in the game. For example, in the standard challenge, there are three different bounces.

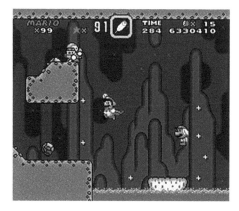

This is the standard challenge for the level. The boulder's bounces depend on the angle of the terrain it lands on. Because of this property, each new challenge in the level will alter the terrain slightly, but those small changes will have big effects for the player. The part of the level that shows it's in the preservation of momentum theme is the sinking platforms seen above. Most of the challenges feature one or two of these. Without them, the player would be able to simply wait for a gap in the boulders, and then move slowly. Because the platforms sink into lava, the player has to rush through and get off the platform before it sinks.

The second challenge evolves the standard by changing the terrain so that Mario has to jump over the oncoming boulder while fighting the angle of the ramp. Getting above the boulders is significantly harder when they're above Mario, rather than beside or below him.

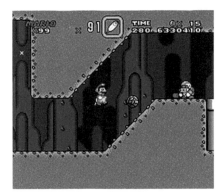 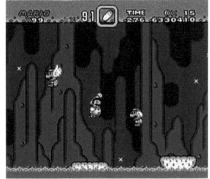

The third challenge, pictured above on the right, brings the sinking platform of the standard challenge back, but both evolved and expanded. Only the back part of the standard challenge expands however; the Chuck disappears entirely. The number of platforms expands from one to three, and the number of Wing Koopas increases from one to two.

The fourth challenge is also tricky to explain. I call this a mutation of the standard because it decreases the qualitative complexity of the challenge greatly, but at the same time performs a normal expansion-by-contraction.

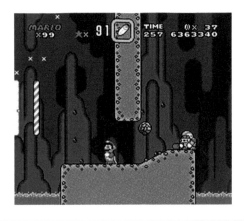

What could be simpler in this cadence than a Digging Chuck with hardly any sloping terrain? At the same time, the critical area to pass through (the aperture in the middle) is contracted. Although this is qualitatively simpler than the standard, it's quantitatively more difficult. My assessment is that, on balance, those two things cancel out. The skill set is the same; the player needs to move through that aperture in one smooth, quick motion at full momentum. The way that skill is employed is just different. Thus, it meets the typical criteria of a mutation.

Challenge five is an evolution of the standard challenge with an extra layer of terrain to complicate the bouncing of the projectile.

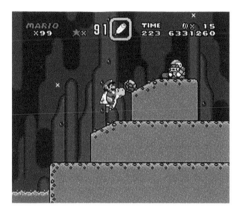

It's quite a bit easier than other challenges in this level because Mario can just run under the Chuck without having to do any jumping (although the player may jump excitedly because they expect to do so), but it still obviously fulfills the preservation of momentum theme.

The sixth and seventh challenges are structurally quite simple. The sixth challenge evolves challenge two by inverting it. Instead of racing up a slope to beat the Chuck's launched dirt, Mario has to race downwards and then leap off the platform before it lands.

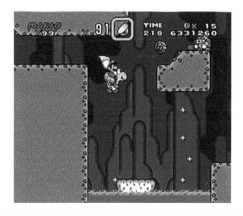

Even if the player is keen to use Yoshi's tongue or the cape to defeat the projectiles, midair attacks are by far the hardest to execute, so it's much easier to just drop and jump quickly to the safe platform on the right. Challenge seven reverses the order of the standard challenge, by leading with a single sinking platform, and then having the player charge up and past (or through) the Chuck waiting at the top.

Again, this is a relatively simple challenge that even reduces some of the delta height of earlier jumps. It totally removes the Wing Koopa and doesn't replace it with anything else, either. I might even call this challenge a de-evolution, rather than a mutation. It's important that not every challenge gets harder; a good cadence requires both upward and downward motion along the axis of obstacles.

The last challenge combines every element in the level into one climactic evolution/expansion.

The long lava pit from challenge three appears first, complete with a necessary enemy-bounce. This leads into the expansion portion of the challenge, where the player has to quickly (because of the sinking platforms and oncoming boulders) get through two consecutive overhead Digging Chucks. To add to this, hitting that springboard quickly enough to avoid the boulder requires hitting it *right away* since the Chuck starts throwing boulders well in advance of Mario being on the platform, and the springboard has a built-in delay. Some credit has to go to the design team though, in that they gave the player a second route through the hardest challenge. Timed correctly, the player can go right past the springboard and cape-glide to the distant platforms under the second Chuck, to the right. It isn't easy, but real, viable options make the hardest challenges less frustrating.

Awesome

In Awesome, every imaginable idea from the preservation of momentum theme is piled up into one level (and in some cases, one challenge). This theme doesn't do a lot of accumulation before this level, but boy does it go crazy with accumulations, now! Toward the end of this level, there are as many as six different iterated ideas from the theme working in each challenge.

The overarching idea that reveals this level's theme is the slippery frozen terrain that preserves Mario's momentum whether the player likes it or not. Back in Donut Secret 2 this idea was matched up with some slow-moving intercepts and small but dangerous pit jumps. Here, the frozen/slippery ground is iterated in a much more diverse way. It starts with a series of valleys; because of the global effect of frozen/slippery ground, even these otherwise simple enemy-filled pits are much more dangerous than they would normally be.

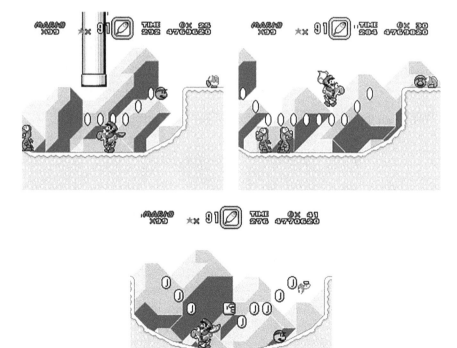

What makes these pits difficult, and what makes the second half of the level difficult as well, is the way the intercepts come towards Mario. If you've read the intercepts theme, you'll know that intercepts so far have mostly fallen into four groups. Some of the intercepts in Awesome don't really fit into any of those categories, especially in context. These Koopa shells have a flight arc that vaguely resembles the Super Koopas in Donut Plains 1 and Butter Bridge 2), but the resemblance isn't close enough that the skills from one translate to the skills of another, especially with the ice in mind. Moreover, the Super Koopas are a medium speed enemy; the Koopa shells travel at max speed. While the player isn't completely unprepared for these situations, it's a lot more challenging than it appears from the picture.

The evolutionary progression of these pits comes in two straightforward sets. The first set consists of these three valleys, which represent a mutation followed by an evolution. You can see here how the pipe bisecting the first valley is removed from the second valley, making a cape-glide possible—but the number of enemies goes up, offsetting some of the ease. (I go back and forth on whether to call this a mutation or not). The first two valleys are the same shape; the third is deeper. This deeper valley retains an element of the first valley, in the coin-block that sits above its lowest point, possibly confining Mario's jumps. The real meat of the evolution, however, is the upgrade from a regular Koopa shell to the rainbow shell. I also count the increased depth of the valley as an expansion because it's much easier for the player to be trapped when having to go so far uphill.

In the second set of challenges, we see the valleys evolve into watery pits. The first pit is not terribly dangerous because so much of the water that Mario could land in is safe from the trajectory of the shell.

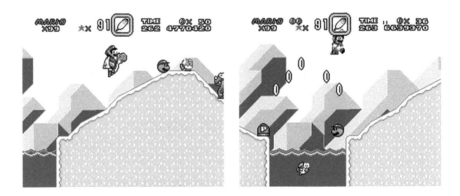

The second watery pit is a combined evolution/expansion. To start, the d-distance in the jump expands. Secondly, there are two intercepts where there used to be one, although the second intercept is now a patrolling fish in the water. But the real hook of this challenge is the p-switch which is a total red herring. Because of the global ice effect, it's much easier for the player to simply bypass this switch and glide across the watery pit rather than trying to hit it, not fall, and then jump onto the transformed coins.

The second half, as I said, is where the challenge goes through the roof (relative to the rest of the game). Throughout this section, the player will be constantly caught between two endless waves of leaping fish. Combined with the ice, it seems as if Mario has no choice but to always be hurrying forward. There's even a star in the first coin-block, if the player somehow knew to bring a Koopa shell to retrieve it (or could nail the Yoshi-dismount jump without taking damage).

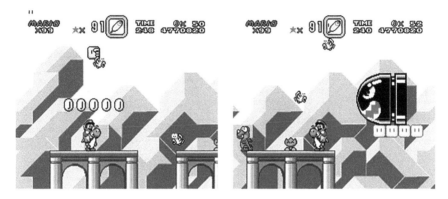

With or without the star, this is an unforgiving section. The endless waves of flying fish take about a half a second to catch up to Mario when he lands on a new platform, meaning that he only has that much time to move to the next platform before he is besieged from both sides again. The first obstacle, the b-standard of the level, is a simple jump to a second platform occupied by a Rex and a fire-flower. The Rex is typical platform fodder, but the fire-flower is just cruel. Even with a star, this section is much easier with the cape powerup, and that exposed fire-flower will can (at least temporarily) take that powerup from Mario. The leap from that platform is even worse as the next platform is obscured by the body of the Banzai Bill for crucial seconds that allow the leaping fish to clutter the skies.

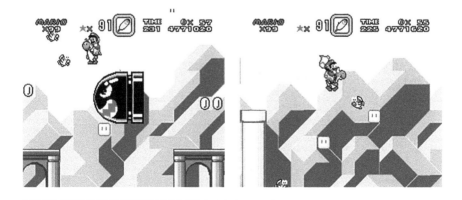

The Banzai Bill problem sees an expansion-by-contraction, as the relevant platform shrinks to one. Fortunately for the players, the Banzai Bill is lower this time and the player can bounce off of it instead of using the platform at all. That bounce is not without its problems, though, as those leaping fish are still going to be soaring around while Mario descends onto the next platform. The next challenge subtracts the Banzai Bill, but expands the number of platforms. The leap from a one-block platform to another one-block platform amidst an endless flood of enemies would be hard enough, but these platforms are also icy.

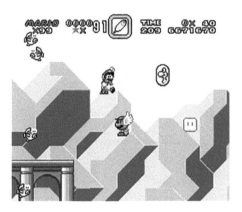

The final challenge is actually somewhat easier, as the Wing Koopa serves as the safest platform in the whole level, making for an easy moving target that can get the player to the final ledge. Technically, this last challenge is an evolution/expansion that substitutes an enemy for a platform and increases the overall d-distance, but the level has been so hard that it can't really find another way to get harder.

Where the pinnacle of the periodic enemies theme was great because it perfectly executed a standard cadence, this level is fascinating because it totally inverts the lessons of the theme. The preservation of momentum theme is all about the virtue of moving quickly to escape obstacles Mario shouldn't even be dealing with. Throughout the theme, there have been an increasing number and variety of obstacles that prevent that rapid movement. Because of the star and because Mario can still plausibly take damage without dying, this level is still fairer than, say, Tubular. It only gets away with being as bizarre as it is because it's both a pinnacle level and located in the Special world.

7

The Intercepts Theme

The intercepts theme is the simplest theme in the game from a design point of view. The reason for this is that placing intercepts is technically easy. Although stacking periodic enemies is conceptually simple, the designer has to account for the interplay of two heterogeneous periods, and allow a window of time in which the player can move or jump. Thus, the math of the periodic enemies theme can get technically difficult for the designer building levels in it. The intercepts theme, on the other hand, isn't about timing; it's about reactions. This fact gives the designer more leeway, and probably made for relatively simple construction. Indeed, the Intercepts theme is one of the architecturally simplest themes in the game, as each level will show. Most levels in this theme are never more architecturally complex than a few platforms at differing heights.

The platforms and jumps themselves are not meant to be difficult; this theme features medium-sized d-distances and delta-heights, but has the largest average platform size for both launching and landing platforms—even larger than those in the preservation of momentum theme. The whole point of this theme is to get Mario into a situation where he's making an architecturally simple jump, and then complicate that jump with intercepts.

What makes this theme easy for the designer but challenging for the player is that levels can become very challenging without much iteration. By Vanilla Dome 4, all the types of intercepts have appeared already, and all that remains for the designer is to mix and match them in a long accumulation phase.

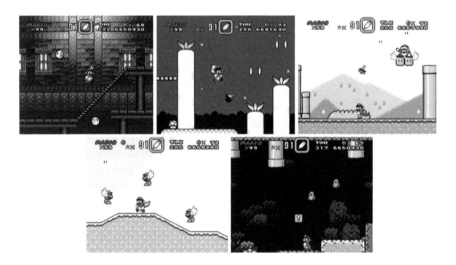

Above, we have the tracking, linear, overhead, bouncing, and swooping intercepts. Not all intercepts are equally difficult. The linear intercept, which is the first to appear, flies in a straight, predictable path, and is often very easy to attack or jump over. The swooping intercept appears next and is a little more difficult because of the bending shape of its flight path. The bouncing or undulating intercept is even more difficult because it changes direction more often. Then finally, the tracking or seeking intercept is the most dangerous because it follows Mario directly, and will adjust its path to collide with Mario. These intercepts don't appear in strict order of difficulty across the game, but the more-difficult intercepts tend to appear less frequently overall, and less frequently in accumulations in particular.

Accumulations are frequent in this theme, and they start early. Butter Bridge 2, for example, has more accumulation content than the pinnacle level of the moving targets theme—but it's only halfway through the game! The pinnacle of the intercepts theme takes the accumulations to a spectacular extreme: *every* kind of intercept appears in that level, usually mixed with several other kinds. During this theme, we'll pay special attention to each unique mix of intercepts, because the combinations are numerous. Yet, every combination manages to provide a new and different challenge.

Donut Plains 2

Donut Plains 2 introduces the intercepts theme in a controlled way, by slowing the scrolling of the level screen down significantly. One of the biggest dangers in the theme comes from Mario running, full speed, into screens the player hasn't seen yet. Once the player is committed to a jump, intercepts that have just appeared on screen can take him or her by surprise. The player probably did that in Donut Plains 1, and was probably hit by the Super Koopas and Pitching Chucks. (Donut Plains 1 isn't in the intercepts theme; it's an introductory level to the cape powerup). This level largely eliminates that danger, because not only is the screen-scroll locked to a specific speed, but the moving floor of the level also frequently interrupts Mario's progress.

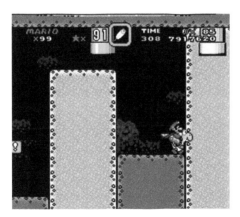

Running into trouble is possible in a few spots, but it's not the level's biggest threat. The other way that this level helps the player to get accustomed to intercepts-based levels is by telegraphing the behavior of the Swooper early, and more than once.

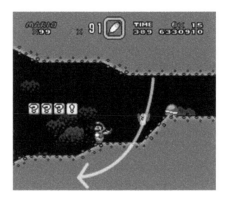

To demonstrate the full flight path of a Swooper without exposing the player to danger, the designers set up the path of this enemy to pass through the floor of the level. This doesn't let the player dealing with the full shape of that arc, but at least it shows the player how the enemy moves.

There isn't a full, organized cadence in this level, but you can see how the first few jumps evolve the same idea by changing the jump distance and shape.

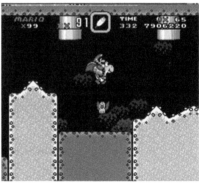

Remember that intercepts are enemies that intersect Mario's flight path when he's already jumping. In this level, the causes of jumps are usually the Buzzy Beetles and rising floors. The Swoopers that come at Mario while he makes those jumps are technically intercepts. These later jumps are only slightly harder than the first one because there's less time to react. The ideas in this level stay very simple and there are not that many jumps in total. They don't add up to a cadence, but they do accomplish their goal of exposing the player to new intercept behaviors.

Donut Secret 1

In a water level, combat changes significantly because Mario is vulnerable from below. Given that this theme is in the action declension, this problem is one the player faces quite often in water levels. The primary intercept in this level is the Rip Van Fish, who will follow Mario after he enters the fish's aggro radius. The Rip Van Fish (hereafter RVF) shares a behavioral property with the Boo: both enemies follow Mario imperfectly. The RVF's flaw is that, as it approaches Mario's position, it tends to "pull up" just a little bit. This built-in error makes evasion possible, but it also makes fighting this fish slightly more difficult for new players who have not yet internalized this property.

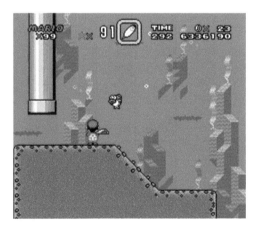

Because players have to either position Mario parallel to a fish (for the cape) or be above them to use fireballs, the first few encounters with RVFs can be tricky. There's probably no better example of a warning shot covering all of a level's elements than this one right here. The first screen introduces the player to every kind of fish and displays their behaviors.

For the rest of the level, the following things will happen: RVFs will seek Mario, Blurps will swim in straight lines, and the white fish will patrol certain spaces. This also highlights just how much the designers accomplished with only three types of enemies: the subsequent challenges provide a decent amount of variety using only what is presented here.

The standard challenge for the level, which you can see below, features an RVF that chases Mario into two other enemies. Now, because of the "pulling up" behavior of the RVF, it will almost certainly overshoot Mario, but new players aren't going to know this yet, and so they'll try to quickly shoot down into the gap.

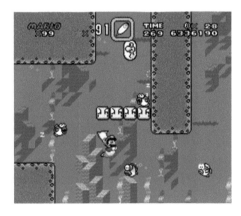

It's this gap that provides the player with a true intercepts-based situation. While swimming, Mario is engaged in one continuous jump. Thus, anytime Mario has to accelerate suddenly (like if he's being chased), anything in his path can serve as an intercept. Thus, these two fish are intercepts in context because Mario is accelerating towards them to avoid the RVF. Fireballs are an easy solution here, but if Mario isn't using that powerup, it's still possible to simply flatten out his path and avoid both enemies. This possibility will disappear in later evolutions.

Next, there is an expansion-by-contraction that brings Mario close to combat, although it's still possible to avoid combat should the player want to choose that path. Indeed, combat is the best solution here, but the low ceiling means that even with fireballs, Mario will have to get in very close to get the right angle to snipe the RVF. If the RVF isn't engaged and defeated, it will chase Mario into these two syncopated Blurps.

By syncopated, I mean any enemies who are parallel and moving at the same speed, but that come at an off-set interval, so that it's clear that Mario is supposed to squeeze between them. (This is something Mario will do frequently in water levels). Because Blurps are so predictable, the gap isn't hard to squeeze through. Once again, Mario is being chased, so speed and reactions are the key skills, and these Blurps serve as intercepts.

The next significant challenge is this one, an evolution/expansion that increases the number of RVFs on screen, and also evolves their positions to surround Mario, making evasion a more complex task.

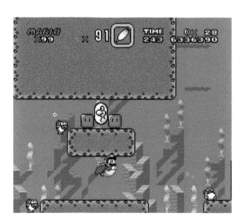

The two patrolling fish on the other end of this challenge aren't any harder than what's come before. The real problem is that the two RVFs could easily follow Mario into the next challenge. That next challenge is a simple expansion-by-contraction of what the player saw two challenges ago. Instead of two Blurps syncopated at four spaces, there are two patrolling fish syncopated two spaces apart. It's also an evolution because unlike the earlier Blurps, these two will double back and damage Mario if he isn't through the gap already.

Subsequently, there is a challenge that is a definite example of the rare de-evolution, but it's one with an interesting purpose. This Blurp is positioned so that the player either must defeat it by combat (which can be tricky because the ceiling makes fireballs difficult here) or must quickly discover how low the "bottom" of the level is. Waiting is an option here, which is part of the reason I call this a de-evolution.

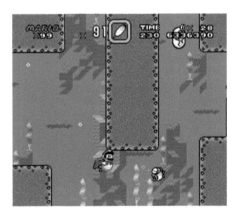

It's interesting that the designers are able to do so much with just one perfectly positioned Blurp, but it's a good object lesson. Not all challenges need to increase in difficulty in a linear fashion, or even increase at all. Sometimes there's a "just right" challenge that can get across a design lesson with a minimum of effort.

The next challenge is a reiteration of the third challenge in this level, with minor changes that don't really constitute an increase in complexity.

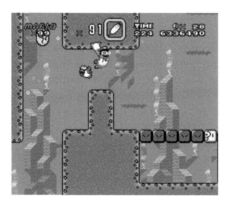

This repetition makes sense only in light of the fact that the player is probably racing forward, trying to get to the hidden key ahead before the P-Block wears off. In that context, a simple challenge works because the player already has enough to focus on.

The next challenge is technically an evolution because it introduces perpendicular patrols. Mario is still being chased by RVFs here, so all four patrolling fish are intercepts by context.

Although technically an evolution, this is easier than many of the earlier challenges in the level. It's usually not the case that levels get easier as they go, but not every level in the game shares one template, either.

Vanilla Dome 4

Vanilla Dome 4 is the only level in the game to use procedural content in a way that actually develops along the lines of a cadence. The "procedure" in question is the procedural generation of bullets that will make the otherwise simple jumps of this level more difficult. In the first half of the level, these bullets come one or two at a time. In the second half of the level, they come five at a time. In the first half of the level, the designers programmed the distribution of the bullets across the screen with a specific philosophy in mind. The basic idea behind their design was that the bullets should intercept where Mario is jumping *to* rather than the platform he is standing *on*. This, of course, reflects the definition of what an intercept is in this game: intercepts don't cause jumps, but rather modify them. For example, if Mario stands at the zero-height mark for the level, he can wait there for the level timer to wind all the way down without ever being hit. Higher up, that would be impossible.

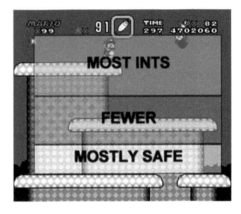

Beyond that, there is no discernible pattern to the way that bullets travel across the screen in the first half of the level. It seems that rather than having to use a different algorithm for each challenge, the designers opted to do the simpler thing and just structure the challenges so that the one algorithm works for several of them.

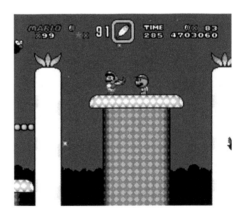

In the standard challenge, Mario leaps over a Koopa, and is intercepted by a bullet from either side. Because Mario is already on a high platform, his jump can take him over both the Koopa and the intercept at once, and the player can use a cape glide to avoid the intercept's path, or come down on top of it. Later challenges evolve this idea by starting Mario lower down, and having him jump into the path of intercepts from below.

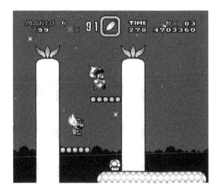 

In these jumps, Mario can be caught mid-flight by a bullet that only just appeared on screen, or by the patrolling Wing-Koopas. There's no way to abort Mario's momentum fast enough to drop below the bullet. Instead, the player has to move him laterally around the bullet, while moving up, which can easily steer him into the Wing Koopas. The spring platforms are also a crucial part of the evolution, as there is a little bit of extra lag-time between the player's jump input and the actual jump on screen. That leaves less time to maneuver while in the air.

The second half of the level is itself an evolution, in which the periodic bullets become something more formidable. Rather than one or two bullets flying across the screen, the second half of the level will shoot five of them at a time. More than just being a greater quantity, these bullets will fly in paths perpendicular to one another, creating some dangerous intersections.

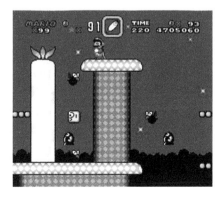

Two things make this challenge much more navigable than it seems at first. The first detail the player should notice is that the bullets always come in the same exact pattern. The second detail to notice is that the bullets only come when Mario stops moving laterally. If Mario remains in the same (laterally measured) two-block space for more than a game-second, the bullets will fire, unless there are still old bullets on screen. This means that this level has introduced a clever crossover challenge that declines toward the preservation of momentum theme. After all, the best way to avoid these bullets is to keep moving, no matter what. The first part of this section obliges this instinct in the player; just look at how flat all those sections are.

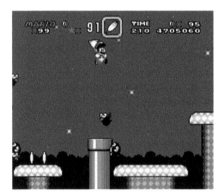 

A subsequent evolution section slows Mario down with springboards.

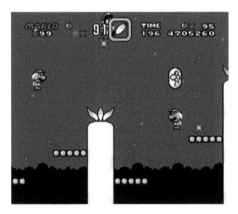

The player has seen the springboards before, but in the context of the five bullets that fire in this half of the level, it's still an evolution. It's a great example of how the context of the new bullet pattern allows the designers to conserve level design ideas and keep the whole thing tight and coherent.

Vanilla Secret 2

Vanilla Secret 2 works as an effective counterpart to Vanilla Dome 4, as it tackles the same design ideas in a different way. Vanilla Dome 4 is all about sending a barrage of intercepts at Mario while he is traversing relatively simple terrain. Vanilla Secret 2 does the same thing, but uses a different kind of intercept—and uses it in greater density. The first half of the level is particularly replete, featuring 25 enemies as densely packed as any in the game. For all their dense packing, though, the challenges are easy to pick apart based on their structure. Moreover, this level shows us some of the nuances of what makes intercepts successful as design features.

An intercept is defined simply as something that modifies Mario's jumps, rather than something that causes Mario's jumps. This means that in any of the challenges below, the first Wing Koopa to come out Mario is the cause of his jump, and everything else is an intercept that interferes with Mario reaching (brief) safety on the ground before the next challenge. The challenges divide up into bunches of Koopas; these bunches are separated by a geographic feature like the crest of a hill, one or more coin-blocks or both.

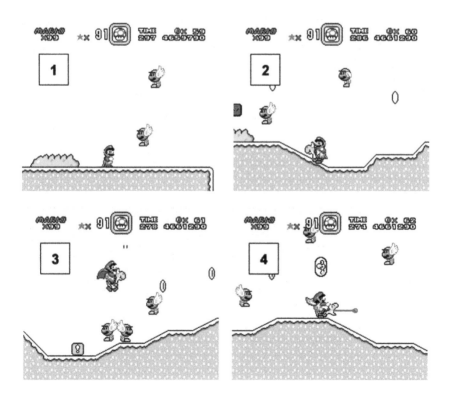

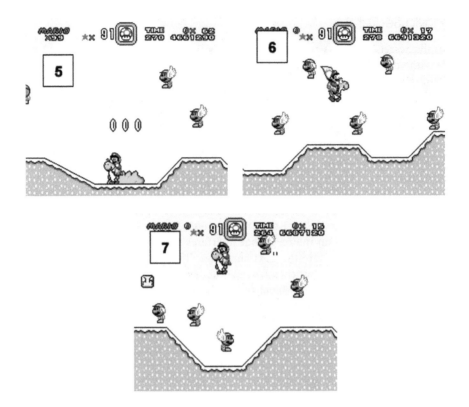

There's a normal progression going on here, although it is highly condensed. The first challenge (1) is the standard challenge that introduces the basic idea in the level: two Wing Koopas that bounce at different heights. The lead Koopa causes Mario to jump; the second Koopa restricts where and how he lands. From there, the progression is fairly simple: challenge (2) expands the number of Koopas, adding another low-bouncing enemy. Challenge (3) begins to mix it up with an evolution in the terran; here we have three low-bouncing Koopas. The reason they're all bouncing low is the shape of the platform below: when high-bouncing Wing Koopas come down a slope, it's very easy to simply walk under them, but low bouncing Koopas are actually harder to face on an up-slope than at any other time. Next, (4) on the way down that same slope the player encounters a mutation, where there are three high-bouncing Koopas who are more dangerous because the down-slope of the hill shortens their bounces. The next challenge (5) is a mutation that reverses the standard challenge to lessen the tension before the bigger challenges coming next. Challenge (6) is another expansion; you can see how it actually still alternates the bounce-pattern of the Koopas in the same way the standard challenge does (low, high, low, high). Challenge (7) expands the number of koopas and adds one evolution to challenge (6), the coin-block on the left causes the Wing Koopas to turn and backtrack, making the center of this challenge a clustery mess if Mario waits too long to get through it. All in all, we have a standard challenge, an expansion, two mutations upon the expansion, a mutation upon the standard challenge, followed by another expansion and finally an evolution—and that's in a really small geographic space, no less.

The second half of the level is broader but less dense, and contains far fewer challenges of any significance. There are some pipe-dwelling Lakitus and Spiny enemies, but they exhibit no particular organization. The reason for this decrease in challenge organization is that this part of the level features algorithmic generation of intercepts, much like Vanilla Dome 4. If Mario stands in one place for more than three in-game seconds, Bob-ombs will parachute down from the top of the screen. The slowness of the parachutes makes these intercepts considerably less fearsome than their counterparts in Vanilla Dome 4, but there is one spot where they can cause trouble. At the end of the level, the final ledge is guarded by a Replicating Chuck. Although this enemy isn't too tough on its own, three Chucks can slow Mario down enough that the Bob-ombs will start to rain down.

These Bob-ombs, plus the Chucks, plus the Lakitu in the pipe throwing Spiny enemies, will quickly add up to an overcrowded screen. This is a great example of an intercepts level declining toward the preservation of momentum theme. Sticking around too long for combat will almost certainly do more harm than good for Mario; it's much better for him to avoid the trap and simply jump and/or bounce his way out quickly.

Cookie Mountain

Cookie Mountain introduces ground-based intercepts. The ground-based intercept is similar to the Boo and Rip Van Fish in that it will usually seek Mario out rather than move in a straight line, but it's also like Bullet Bills and Wing Koopas in that it can—and often should—be defeated by jumping on it. Technically, the player has already seen one kind of ground-based intercept in the Rainbow Shell that begins Donut Plains 4, and the Monty Moles have appeared before, too. This is the first level that uses ground-based intercepts in a thematic way, however, and it teaches new players the enemy behaviors and skills they need to know going forward. The ground-based intercept that this level focuses on is the Monty Mole. The Monty Mole has two particularly important behaviors that the player needs to be aware of.

The level immediately makes it clear that the Monty Mole enemy will leap out of the ground to a height of four blocks before seeking out Mario. These enemies are not hard once on the ground, but they're tricky (at least to new players) while they're launching. The designers give the player a warning shot in the first screen, when the level loads. Other moles will only fire when Mario gets close, making them harder to react to.

The standard challenge for the level comes immediately after, the first few moles: this Monty Mole will leap up from the ground so quickly that it's very nearly impossible to run past him without taking damage. Mario will need to jump because of the Mole, and herein lies the problem. The Monty Mole isn't done once he's out of the ground; the fact that he (and his buddies—he almost always comes in groups) will continue to chase Mario means that Mario's jump has to be modified. It doesn't always have to be modified to avoid immediate damage, but the player wants to avoid landing only one or two blocks from a mole that can then run up and damage him before he can jump again.

The warning sign (disturbed earth) that the Monty Moles use can trick new players into slowing Mario down. This causes a problem when the Mole is at or above Mario's level because, if his momentum is lost, jumping over the Moles will be harder. Moles can jump as high as four blocks into the air, and from a standstill it's not easy to ascend to five blocks in height quickly enough to get on top of the Mole. Thus, the player's reactions have to either anticipate the Mole's flight path or aim to leap beyond it. Most of the challenges in this level have to do with making it harder and harder for the player to do just that.

The next challenge is an evolution challenge, but it's an odd one. In this evolution the player meets—for the first time in the game—the Sumo Brother. The Sumo Brother is capable of making the ground below him catch on fire, radiating out from a center point. That radiating pattern will often make players want to edge forward rather than be overtaken by the fire.

The Sumo Brother forms one side of a trap. On the other side of the Sumo Brother's damage field is a buried Monty Mole. Because of the low ceiling, the player has a good chance of reacting badly and either touching the fire or getting hit by the mole. It's odd that the designers would introduce a whole new enemy just to make an evolution challenge, though. It's even odder that this enemy would only appear in two levels. Whether he was easy to program and animate, and the designers simply kept him for this reason, I don't know. He does see more development in this level, however.

The next challenge is a simple challenge that helps to demonstrate the Monty Mole's ability to follow Mario's movements. With the shell located just before it, this challenge isn't hard by any means, but it does tell the player a lot about the Monty Mole's behavior.

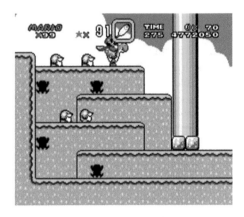

Although the most important property of the Moles is their explosive arrival, their seeking behavior is important as well (and is good training for dealing with Wigglers, later). In close quarters, Moles are quick enough to do damage if the player isn't paying close attention.

After that, we see the real shape of the challenges to come: an evolution/expansion that pits Mario against multiple Moles springing out of different heights and in greater quantities. Not only are the heights different, but the Moles' emergence is also staggered in time so that some will be on the ground and some in the air.

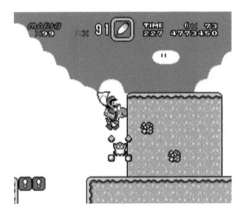

The mixed heights and timings are further complicated by the platform above, which allows the Moles to drop down, potentially onto Mario's head. The first problem, though, is that the player can only reliably land Mario on the two blocks of space between the bottomless pit and the first Mole. The second problem is having to jump again immediately, and not knowing where to go with all the various Moles coming out. The tracking/seeking property and staggered bursts also wreak havoc during a cape glide that would otherwise be useful here.

Following that, there is an obvious expansion upon the first Sumo Brother challenge, in which there are now two Brothers raining down fire, and a Mole filling the exact same role as before. The music note blocks aren't a substantive enough change to call this anything except an expansion.

While a higher ceiling does make it harder to attack the Sumo Brothers, it also means it takes longer for their bolt of energy to strike the ground and cause a fire. Knowing how quickly that bolt came down in the last challenge, it seems to make sense that the designers gave the player more breathing room with two Brothers on the screen at once.

After this, there is one of the game's most obvious expansions: the Moles spring from the cliff-side much as before, but in an obviously greater quantity.

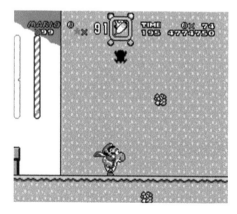

Despite the resemblance, this doesn't evolve the previous challenge because there aren't any platforms overhead for the Moles to run along, meaning that they'll always land right below their pop-out points. After this is another relatively straightforward challenge.

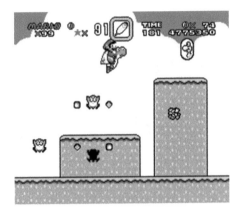

This is a mutation upon the first cliff full of staggered Moles: it reconfigures the Monty Mole population in a different (but not more complex) way.

The end of the level has a couple of slightly bizarre—although not necessarily bad—design choices. The first one is the roulette block. Most of the time, when the roulette block appears, it's followed by a dense gauntlet of enemies, so it's clear that the point of the roulette block was to give the player a Super Star. This Roulette Block is followed by a grand total of three enemies, so the reason for its presence is not clear. Irrespective of powerups from that block, this challenge is unusual. Here the designers have created an evolution of an evolution, but have removed the standard challenge element from it.

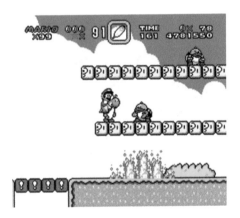

Up until this point in the level, the Sumo Brothers have always interacted in a meaningful way with the Monty Moles that accompany them. This time there are no Moles, but there is an evolution that stacks the brothers on top of one another. Levels usually don't drop their main mechanic for the last challenge. In this case, I think the designers had nothing left to do with the Monty Mole, but needed an impressive challenge with which to end the level.

Butter Bridge 2

Butter Bridge 2 feels big, open, and chaotic, but it is very organized. Much of the feeling of freedom comes from the fact that the level is very flat and so offers the player some opportunities to soar up into the sky. This is one of the few levels where flying over everything with the cape is inadvisable. The higher levels of the sky can still be filled with flying enemies, and the high number of enemies on the ground makes descent equally dangerous. Unless the player can sustain flight for the whole level (a technique that will break almost any level in the game), the player is better off not soaring up there. Although this is probably just serendipity, it's nice to see that there were levels that offered some unexpected peril to players using sustained flight.

If the player isn't constantly soaring up and down with the cape, he or she will actually encounter one of the most neatly organized levels in the entire game. In fact, this level is so well organized that it could be used as a model for teaching the Nintendo style of design. It has all of the classic features, beginning with a clear warning shot and followed by a standard challenge.

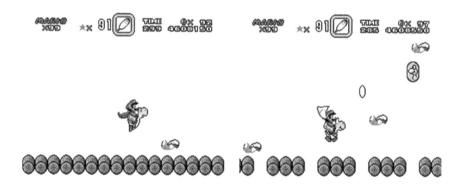

The standard challenge gives way to these small evolution/expansions pretty quickly. The goal of this challenge is to prepare the player for the speed and arc of the Super Koopa. Although this level is brimming with them, the Super Koopa isn't a terribly common enemy in the rest of the game. Moreover, this enemy travels at a speed not shared with many other intercepts (about halfway between a projectile and a Wing Koopa).

The evolutions start to come once the gaps in the bridge close up and the player faces one long section filled with intercepts. The first thing the player encounters is the "B" element that will become part of the many A+B evolutions to come. From there, it's not hard to spot the evolutions and expansions that follow. The number of kicked Koopa Shells goes up, as does the number of swooping Super Koopas.

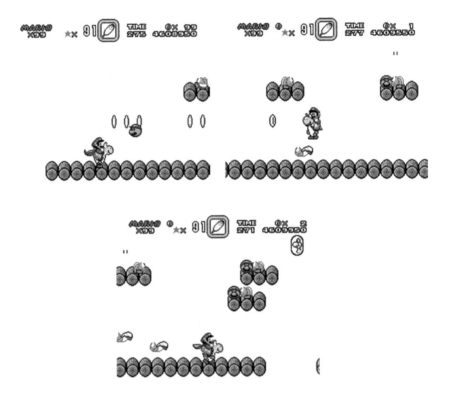

What you see above is the hallmark of the second half of the intercepts theme: it's all about mixing types of intercepts. When intercepts are mixed, the player has to choose (very quickly) which enemy will cause Mario to jump, and which enemy then becomes the modifying intercept; sometimes this choice is ambiguous. This adds a cognitive layer to an otherwise twitchy reaction skill. The obvious mix is the A+B evolution in which the player has to react to both a kicked shell and a Super Koopa, on the left, above. This is succeeded, however, by an A+B+C evolution, in which another Super Koopa with a red cape launches from the ground with an entirely different arc, adding yet another intercept with a different flight path to the challenge. (Note that the Super Koopas will start coming down all over this zone on a timer-based algorithm, so the exact number can be confusing. With that in mind, there are also deliberately-placed enemies that do not run on an algorithm, and it is based on these that the challenges are divided).

The second section of this level moves away from mixing enemy types and instead throws various configurations of Super Koopas, in different shapes and quantities, at Mario. This section of the level is also filled with algorithmically generated Super Koopas, who will emerge from both edges of the screen and fly toward Mario. The pattern of those Super Koopas is only meaningful in that they make everything else an intercept. That is, if Mario is always jumping and avoiding them, then literally any other enemy on screen becomes a modifying intercept. What makes the section really work, though, is that layered on top of this procedural barrage are the hand-touched challenges that cause the player to use a variety of skills. The first such challenge is this wall of intercepts.

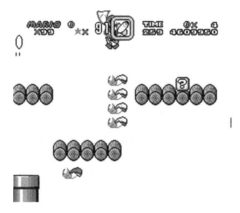

Although Super Koopas come in stacks in most levels they're in, they're never this tightly packed. This density serves to make the stack shorter, but it also prevents Mario from having any useful action solutions. The best a player can do is to defeat one or two of these Koopas as they swoop down, and the remaining Koopas will probably damage Mario. Jumping over the stack is probably a better idea, and it's certainly easy to do if Mario is on that upper platform (above, left). From the bottom platform, it's much harder.

The next set of challenges is far more effective because Mario has no alternatives. Here, two Super Koopas fly down, leaving Mario a gap between them to jump through. The bottom Koopa is the cause of the jump, and the top Koopa is the intercept.

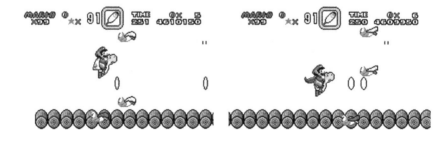

Following that is a logical expansion-by-contraction. The gap between the Koopas narrows, and the jump becomes significantly more difficult.

In the end, the overall structure of the level takes the player from the "here comes a speeding enemy" set of challenges to a "how am I going to thread this gap" set of challenges. The former is based on reacting as quickly as possible to get airborne (or run forward and duck, alternatively) and away from enemies, while the second is about moving towards those enemies in order to get the best position between them. Both involve lots of mid-air adjustments and quick movements, and so they're both clearly intercept situations.

Forest of Illusion 1

Forest of Illusion 1 begins to mix ground-based intercepts with enemies of other kinds. Thus far, most intercepts have been aerial. In Cookie Mountain, the game started showing the player the ways in which ground-based enemies can be intercepts, too, but the Monty Mole also has an aerial component. Like the rare rainbow-shell and the slightly more common Monty Mole, the star of this level, the Wiggler, will follow Mario and thus become an intercept, especially in the presence of other enemies.

After taking jump damage, the Wiggler will speed up rather than dying, and will chase Mario more aggressively. The lone Wiggler shown above is the standard challenge, and isn't really an intercept because it's so easy to avoid. This will change with evolutions.

The first evolution of the standard challenge adds other types of enemies. These Goombas don't leave useful Koopa shells, and so won't give Mario any way to defeat the nearby Wiggler. This means that Mario will have to steer around it if he's not using Yoshi.

The second and third evolutions are different in a meaningful way. The springboard jump seen below is complicated by the fact that if Mario doesn't launch quickly, the Wiggler with its odd hitbox and bounce properties can interrupt Mario's attempt.

 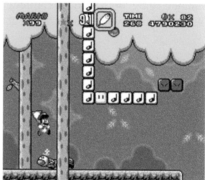

The third evolution adds a ceiling above the Wiggler and the chance for a 1-up if Mario can use the note-blocks the right way while avoiding the Wiggler. All of these challenges are clearly evolutions that increase the complexity of the standard challenge, but they're so different from one another that they can't be called mutations of each other.

After a simple expansion, the challenges in this level begin to grow in size and complexity, building off the second challenge's combination of a Wiggler and other mixed enemies. First, there's a simple expansion that adds two Wigglers.

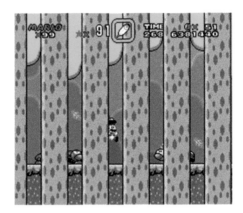

Three damaged Wigglers will make for an unsafe platform, necessitating Mario's quick exit. By that same token, the jump attacks that make Wigglers dangerous also allow the player to chain together several jumps while preserving Mario's momentum. Hints of the preservation of momentum theme continue in the next few evolution challenges. There are two long challenges that evolve the level's first evolution again. Both sections combine ground intercepts with air intercepts, by having ground-based enemies drop out of the sky.

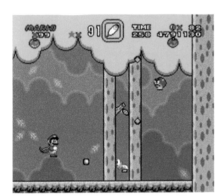
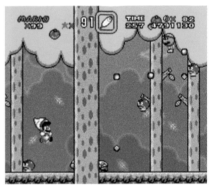

The buildup of enemies on the ground, including Wigglers, puts Mario in a situation where he needs to either keep enemy-bouncing, or go all-out with combat techniques like using Yoshi and/or the Koopa shells available. The falling enemies add another layer of intercepts to the mix in both locations, often staggered in close proximity to one another so as to intercept Mario's downward arc after any jump. The terraced structure of the second long challenge (below) complicates this even more, by contracting the area that Mario has available for dodging.

7. The Intercepts Theme

Both of these are sections full of mixed intercepts, a trend that becomes more frequent after this level. (Although both these sections can be played as a preservation of momentum challenge if the player gets the Super Star from the slot block before it). After those two long challenges, the final evolution in the level adds a Flyin' Hammer Brother. This time though, he is the B portion of an A+B evolution that includes the Wiggler.

What the designers were probably aiming for here is either to get Mario bouncing off the Wiggler into the Hammer Brother's platform, or to make the player use the additional height of an enemy-bounce off the Wiggler to get over the right-hand wall. While this serves well as a pinnacle challenge for the level, it doesn't actually build on the two previous evolutions; rather, it goes back and builds on the second challenge in the level. If every evolution challenge in a level were another step up the chain of complexity, levels would become too challenging and needlessly cluttered. In this challenge, the designers show us how to create a good, sufficiently climactic challenge without having to throw everything in the level into one challenge.

Forest of Illusion 3

Forest of Illusion 3 is the purest example of the intercepts theme, and yet it doesn't feel like most intercepts-themed levels. The reason for this is that in stripping away everything that isn't an intercept, the level takes away the defining experience of the intercepts theme. The intercepts theme is about obstacles that complicate jumps; this level is full of that, but everything else typical to an intercepts level (like jump-causing regular enemies) is removed. In the entire level, there is only one enemy that behaves like a normal enemy, while everything else behaves like an intercept. The cause of all this is a bubble.

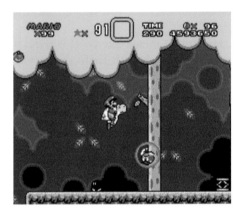

When it collides with any object, this bubble will burst and drop an enemy out of the sky and possibly onto Mario. The problem with this is that instead of looking at the platforms ahead, the player is going to have to spend all of his/her attention on looking at what's above Mario, to make sure that there won't suddenly be a Bob-omb or Goomba falling from a coin-block. The constant threat of possible falling objects and extra attention paid to the sky necessitates the removal of anything ground-based. Thus, the designers left out things like Wigglers and Koopas.

That's only half the story, though; the other half is that one of the objects a bubble can collide with is Mario, and when this happens, it stops his momentum entirely. When taking enemy damage in flight, Mario does usually lose some momentum, but the effect is enhanced when he collides with a bubble. After hitting a bubble, Mario tends to drop like a rock, at least for a second, before the player can cape-glide again. To make this effect more meaningful in gameplay, the bubbles are frequently positioned to intercept Mario's jump-path where it would cause him to take damage or die.

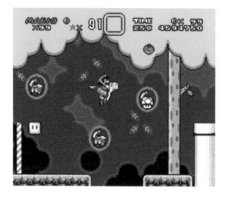

The bubble containing the Mushroom pictured here doesn't cause damage by itself, but it can drop Mario straight into the pitfall below. In the second case, on the right, Mario's jump is delayed to the very edge of the pit because of the cluster of bubbles which would hurt and possibly kill him. The entire level is rife with this.

The expansions are somewhat obvious; the number of bubbles gradually increases across the early challenges of the level. Because of the free-floating nature of these bubbles, it's tough to pin down a single place where there is an evolution. What evolves is the aerial terrain, rather than the enemies that occupy it.

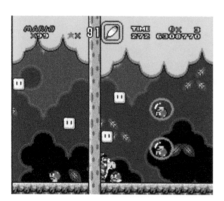

The level progresses from a fairly typical pipe geography to a scattering of overhead blocks which pop the enemy bubbles, and then from there to a much thicker scattering of overhead blocks, and finally to a scattering of blocks with a Charging Chuck thrown in. There aren't really "point" evolutions, but the overall trend is clear. Throughout the level, the player will constantly have to react to unusual enemy patterns and take modified jump-paths because of the clouds of bubbles. The designers set out to create an environment where every situation called only for the player's intercept-specific skills, and they accomplished just that.

The Ghost Houses

We're going to look at all of the ghost houses at once. One of my reasons for doing this is that it's probably best to ignore the puzzles and secrets in the levels, as there isn't really a repeatable lesson to be learned from them. Almost all of the puzzles are simple things that become uninteresting immediately after the player figures them out. *Zelda* titles are the place to go if you want to study Nintendo's puzzles in a meaningful way. Another reason for doing all the Ghost Houses in one shot is that these levels feature very few challenges per level, and those that they do feature are so similar to one another that there's hardly any point in separating them. Challenges in one Ghost House tend to act like evolutions upon challenges in earlier Ghost Houses, rather than evolutions within the progression of the level itself. For example, this challenge is from Vanilla Dome, and it uses the ghosts' mechanics nicely:

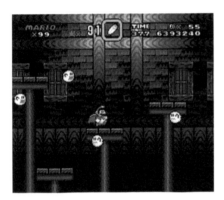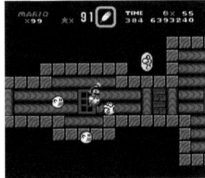

On the left, you can see how this setup makes the scattered Boos into a meaningful challenge. As the Boos close in on Mario, the player can jump around the various platforms to evade. This will also show the player the hidden property of the Boos: they don't fly straight at Mario, but rather will pull up a bit. The Forest Ghost House evolves this by putting a ceiling on the level, and then bisecting the safe space by adding an Eerie. In Vanilla Ghost House, it's easy to take advantage of the staggered platforms because there are many of them and Mario can jump through the floors when ascending. In Forest Ghost House, the player faces a more difficult version of those circumstances.

While it takes until the Vanilla Dome for the designers to create a challenge that really exposes the Boos' behavior, the Big Boo gets a more effective introduction. In Donut Secret Ghost House, this challenge does a lot to teach the player how to handle Big Boos, and by extension, Boos in general:

Here, the springboard clues the player in to the notion that they need to draw the Big Boo down to a height where the springboard's additional momentum will be enough to clear him. Even the newest players know what a springboard does. Thus, the deduction that the Big Boo's height needs to be drawn down is easy enough, and it will reveal this essential behavior. That said, I don't think the exposure to Big Boos that begins in this level adequately prepares the player for the Big Boo boss, who behaves in a much different way. Throughout the first few ghost houses, it seems like the designers categorically treated Boos as though the player would already remember how to deal with them from *Super Mario Bros. 3*. Although they are a simple class of enemy, I don't think this was necessarily a wise philosophy.

The enemies in ghost houses are almost all intercepts, and while the Boos are not always interesting intercepts, many of the other enemies are. The Eerie enemy sees the most development of any enemy in the ghost houses, and they accomplish the inherent goals of the intercepts theme most adeptly. The Eerie is a fast enemy; its speed is exactly calibrated so that it's not that dangerous if Mario is walking or stopped, but it becomes a real challenge to a new player's reflexes if Mario is running at full momentum. What makes the Eerie interesting from a design point of view, however, is its variety of movement patterns.

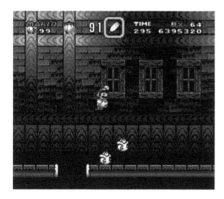 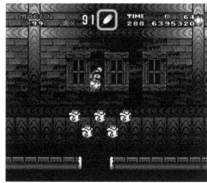

Here, the Eeries force the player to minutely alter the shape of Mario's jumps, with a degree of subtlety that will be essential in the later part of the game. In each case, the Eerie isn't necessarily the cause of the jump, but rather just the factor that shapes the jump once it is begun. Thanks to the Fishin' Boo (an evolved form of the Fishin Lakitu from Forest of Illusion 4), these challenges emphasize the controlled-height jump in a way that the player will clearly pick up on.

The Fishin' Boo isn't the only instance of a Ghost enemy acting as an evolution of an enemy first found outside a ghost house; in two ghost house levels (Vanilla Ghost, Valley Ghost), there is the anonymous green glob, which is a rather sly evolution of an enemy one might not expect. It's a kind of mid-range enemy that has a flight path splitting the difference between Swoopers and Super Koopas.

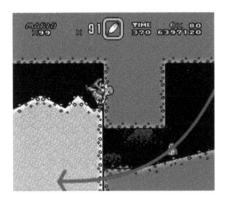 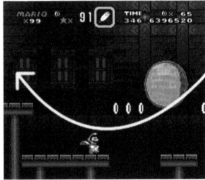

The flight path of the green glob, Super Koopa and Swooper are similar; so much so that they usually elicit similar strategies from the player in the form of cape-glides and back-jumps. One could argue that the green globs are part of the same idea as the swooping swarm of ghosts in the second section of Forest Ghost House or the beginning of Donut Ghost House, but those only look similar and have a similar setting—they don't require similar skill sets.

It seems that the mission of the Ghost Houses was to intersperse short, puzzle-oriented levels into the course of the game, and they have obviously succeeded at doing that. The puzzles, especially the final puzzle in Valley of Bowser, are not terrible. But while much of what goes on in this game can be translated to other games, the puzzles in the Ghost Houses don't really reveal an interesting intersection between mechanics, or a consistent and exportable strategy. For those reasons, studying them wouldn't enrich our understanding of this game more than a simple FAQ or walkthrough would.

Chocolate Island 1

Chocolate Island 1 introduces the Dino Rhino and the Dino Torch, which is an evolved ground-based intercept. In fact, the level does little else than introduce this enemy because of how dynamic it can be in the right situation. The Dino Rhino and its little version, the Dino Torch, include the accumulated properties of numerous enemies up to this point. Like the Rex, they (or at least the big ones) take two hits to defeat. Like the Wing Goomba, they bounce/leap. Like the Wiggler and Monty Mole, they follow Mario across the map. Unlike any other enemy, they will jump over obstacles three blocks in height or less to follow and/or surprise a waiting Mario. Lastly, the little one breathes fire.

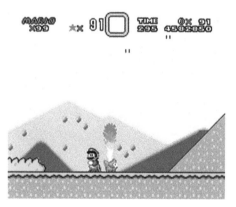

Because of all these properties, the Dino is the level's only real feature; except for one spot in the middle, all the challenges are just changes in the shape of the terrain. These properties are enough, especially within this skill theme. The novel, ranging behaviors of the Dinos make for a lot of instances where the player will have to suddenly turn, jump or glide in a new direction. That's what the intercept theme is about, and these enemies do a very good job of making that kind of player behavior happen by themselves.

In addition to the fact that everything in the level is built around one enemy, or perhaps because of that fact, the challenge structure is a little unusual. This level is best understood as two standard challenges, one being a set of slanted platforms with Dinos on it, and one being a shaped valley with several more of them in it.

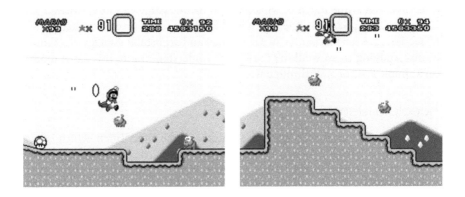

Both of these see iteration: the valley geography mutates (being neither harder nor easier, just a little bit different, qualitatively) and the number of Dinos goes up. What's odd about this is that the number of Dinos goes all the way up to its maximum (4) in the level immediately, rather than slowly building across multiple challenges.

The later mutation which changes the shape of the valley keeps the same number of enemies. The sudden surge of enemies and lack of meaningful fluctuation within this progression is unusual. Then again, this level is all about exposing the player to this enemy in large numbers so that the crowded terrain forces the player to intercept-style reactions and redirections.

The pinnacle of the level is another terrain evolution. This time, the relatively smooth valleys are replaced by this section of pipe-enclosed ditches which make it harder to avoid the enemies. Because the pipes make it so that Mario must jump, the player will feel the intercept quality of the enemies here the most vividly.

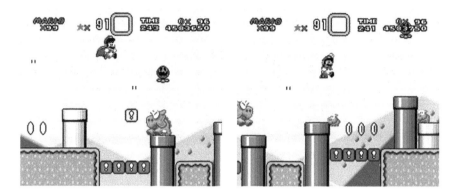

Between the many Dinos that jump over the pipes (effectively increasing the pipes' height) and follow Mario as he moves through the challenge, and the Pumpkins that also leap up, this is a fairly dense challenge. With the switch palaces, the penalty is low, but the challenge is so long that Mario can easily take damage twice and die just from the enemies. This is probably the best evidence for the player's awareness of the increasing threat of intercepts as they accumulate at the end of this theme.

Star World 2

Like many of the other levels in the Star Road and Special zones, Star World 2 does something a little bit weird. In this case, the weirdness is simplicity in a game that rarely does anything simple. This level is simply a "gonzo" water level, featuring incredibly sparse level architecture and numerous swarms of fish-type enemies. There are some expansions at work, as you can see the gaps between groups of fish drop.

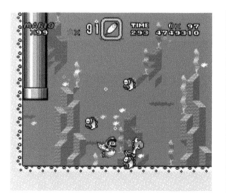

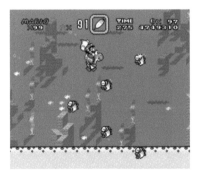

There are two kinds of intercepts (seeking, linear) that mutate a few different ways. The numbers change a little, but there's no clear upward trend. Except for the second spear of Blurps, none of these waves can properly be called expansions. We also can't call them evolutions because nothing new is added, and there's never an A/B mashup. The shapes and positions of the fish do change, though, so it does make for different, mutated views of the same challenge.

The only other design feature of note is one only found one time elsewhere: if the player is able to make it to the first coin-block while still under the effects of the star powerup, this block will issue a second star. This conditional mechanic is only featured in one other level—that being Donut Secret 2. That said, this mechanic is used numerous times in Yoshi's Island, in the Baby-Mario version of the star. Perhaps these two levels were the genesis of that idea.

Sunken Ghost Ship

Although this level is short and does not have a real cadence, it nevertheless reveals some useful techniques. The free-fall section is a quintessential example of reward-by-fun, executed perfectly. There's actually not much to say about it other than that the combination of a Super Star and the uncertainty below makes for just the right amount of tension for a reward-by-fun. The two sections before the free-fall have a lot more to teach us. This pop-in cloud of Boos seems dangerous, but it isn't for an important reason.

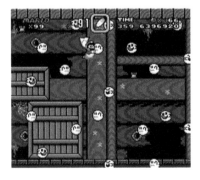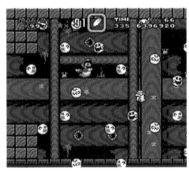

Although the cloud of Boos comes on suddenly and fills most of the screen, it is not dangerous because the Boos have been modified: their hitboxes are smaller. In the image above and left, Mario is not in the act of taking damage; he can pass through the outer portions of the Boos without any trouble. The center of any given Boo will still damage him, but the "soft" hitbox means that the player can react to the appearance of the ghosts and steer elsewhere in the water. This, of course, is the kind of reaction-based situation that indicates the presence of intercepts. These intercepts don't behave like the other intercepts in the game, but that is what makes them noteworthy. It's almost a shame this section doesn't see more development in a short cadence. Above (right), it's obvious how the designers might have done it, by adding undulating enemies like the Eerie, but one evolution is all that occurs. The goal here seems to have been an interesting introduction to a symbolically important reward-by-fun section. Too much length will kill a reward-by-fun, and so we see one of the many places in which designers have to compromise an interesting but untested idea to meet another limitation.

Valley of Bowser 2 (First Section)

Although the largest section of this level is in the periodic enemies theme, the first section features a developed cadence in the intercepts theme. This cadence is a bit short (although rather dense), but it does develop clearly and with all the normal features of a typical theme. It also features some unique intercept combinations, as it brings back the disused Swooper. The standard challenge sets up a moving floor that carries Mario over an otherwise impassable wall. When Mario rides the platform to its apex, a Swooper flies from an invisible position above the screen and cuts across Mario's path. Specifically, that path cuts off Mario's ability to jump from wall to wall, avoiding the rising floor in the middle.

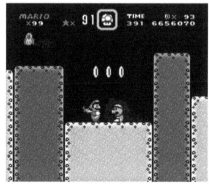

This Swooper/platform combo evolves quickly across the cadence, combining with various other enemies. The first instance is a simple evolution that adds a patrolling Koopa, with another invisible Swooper waiting for Mario above the platform to the right. The next challenge is another evolution/expansion. There are now three enemies, two of them definitely intercepts, and two platforms.

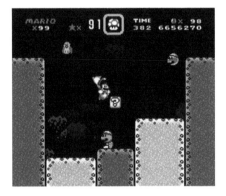

The Swooper also moves from its normal position atop the platform, and instead appears in the middle of the challenge. The point of this is to prevent Mario from just gliding across the gap, as his path will be cut off by the Swooper's arc. This means a lot, since that rainbow shell makes getting through the valley between platforms quite difficult. The rainbow shell is a moderately dangerous enemy, but when it's coming at Mario from above or in a confined space, its danger is enhanced considerably. Both of those things are true here, making this the clear climax of the cadence.

After this, the challenges actually devolve a bit, although they're still more complex than the standard challenge.

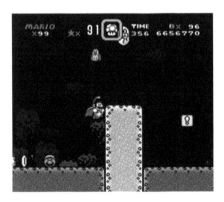

There are several Koopas to deal with, but the Swooper is still the most dangerous element. Although it's not in the most typical structure, this section features a clear and fully developed cadence that makes a long level that much longer. If the section that came after it weren't so bad (see the write-up in periodic enemies theme), this would be a much more memorable level for having sections in different themes.

Outrageous

Outrageous is the climax of the intercepts theme, and it delivers on its climactic potential much like the other pinnacle levels, while at the same time doing something totally brilliant and unique. The general structure of Outrageous is to simply take every kind of intercept in the game and combine them in various ways. As the various intercepts start to overlap, their combined behaviors make for some very tricky challenges. Because there are so many different kinds of intercepts, it would be impossible (from both a design and technical perspective) to get them all into one challenge, although several places in this level come close. In order to do as much as possible, this level has one cadence embedded inside another cadence, something which really isn't done anywhere else in this game.

The level begins simply enough, by showing a standard challenge of one ground-based intercept, the Wiggler. To this it adds a new enemy which is unique to this level, the Bound Fire, in a simple A+B evolution.

 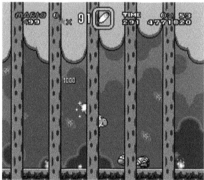

Although the enemies are clearly both ground-based intercepts, their behavior is different enough that the combination is complex. The Bound Fires move periodically, with a "hopping" motion that takes them above ground height, and they leave flames in their wake. Although it's possible to defeat the flames in combat, they're small enough that it isn't easy, especially when there are other intercepts around. One thing this challenge teaches the player is how to "surf" the Wiggler to stay mobile and out of low-lying danger. Those two challenges represent the standard challenge and its first evolution.

This brings us to the cadence-within-a-cadence. The section pictured below is defined by the cannons that shoot Bullet Bills.

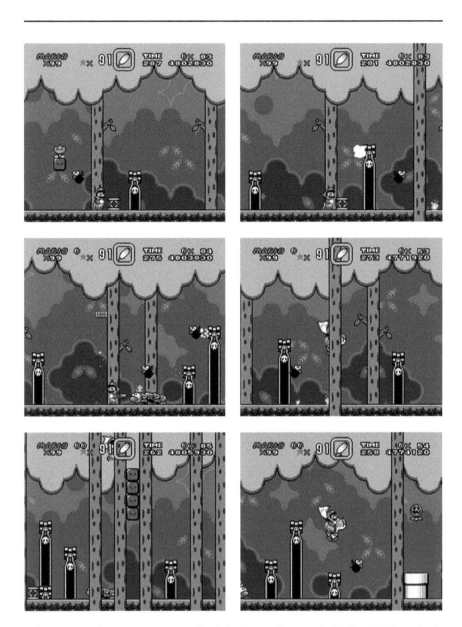

What you see here is a new standard challenge (the single Bullet Bill launcher), followed by a series of expansions and evolutions. Each evolution is demarcated by the presence of one higher-than-average turret or other obstacle that prevents Mario from easily gliding from turret to turret. The pattern seems clear enough: every new "room" between two cannons features a new combination of enemies. Take careful note that the number of guns actually goes up too. In challenge one, there's only one gun, but for every challenge after, there are guns both behind and in front of Mario, and they are equally dangerous. What's more, the guns don't fire at the same time or at obvious intervals, so there's almost no way for the player to simply "figure out" the pattern and focus on something else. Indeed, because Mario has to carry the springboard through several challenges, the player has to focus on that puzzle instead. This is the intercepts theme at its most idiosyncratic. Intercepts are what happen when the player is trying to focus on something else and has to react. To create the pinnacle challenge for this theme, this embedded cadence pulls together every kind of intercept and then makes Mario extra vulnerable by putting a springboard in his hands.

The reason I say that the Bullet Bill section truly is an embedded cadence is that, after the shooting stops, the level resumes almost as if the previous few challenges had never happened. The guns become a minor part of the subsequent challenges, and the level starts sequentially introducing various kinds of intercepts before accumulating them again. The level begins by introducing the Hammer Brother and breakout/drop intercepts.

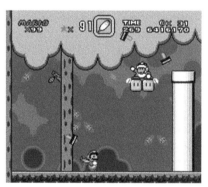

This all builds to an obvious second pinnacle that combines as many kinds of intercepts as will fit in the level for technical reasons.

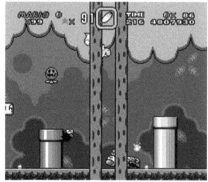

Each image above shows some kind of accumulation involving Hammer Brothers, Bullets, Wigglers, and Bound Flames, with all of them (except the flames) coming together in a rather cramped pinnacle challenge. While that island is cramped, it's still easier to jump out of than the earlier embedded climax, so I would deem this a slightly lesser—but still definitive—second climax for the level.

What's amazing about this level is how oddly structured it is, yet how well this odd structure works. The embedded cadence isn't merely a digression, it's the climax of the level—and yet it comes well before the architectural mid-point of the level! It's a rare structure in game design. There are two pinnacle challenges, both built out of an accumulation strategy that makes this level difficult but fair. Nothing appears in the level which isn't totally normal for the theme, and both pinnacle challenges only contain ingredients found earlier in the level. Within the framework that *Super Mario World* has set up, this is an impressive feat.

8

The Mini-Theme & Isolated Concepts

Mini-Theme: Vertical Levels (Vanilla Secret 1, Gnarly)

Excluding water levels, there are not that many sections in *Super Mario World* that feature vertical progression, where Mario has to go upwards instead towards a goal of moving left to right. We've already covered the levels that feature a fence-like mesh, mostly as sub-sections of the periodic enemies theme. Generally, those levels don't develop with any clear pattern. Part of the problem with vertical levels may be that the mechanics of the game allow only a small amount of possible content. Compared to its historical peers, *Super Mario World* was overflowing with game mechanics, enemies, environments, and player abilities. Yet, the vertical levels in *Super Mario World* show where the design team scraped up against the edges of their design. The two levels in this mini-theme are Vanilla Secret 1 and Gnarly, which have a lot in common. The second half of Morton's castle is also a vertical climb, but it fits into the moving targets theme very well and has little in common with the two levels analyzed below.

What the design team found in vertical levels is that they make for interesting open mazes. By this, I mean that in both these levels, there aren't too many walls because gravity does the work of a wall in preventing Mario from reaching certain parts of the level. The best example of this in Vanilla Secret 1 is this section, where the player needs to move a springboard to the right location in order to access an obvious but distant pipe.

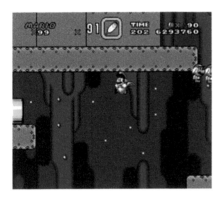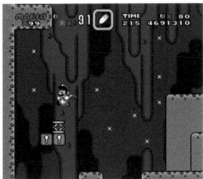

As it is in many other places, it's possible for an experienced player to "cheat" with the cape and reach this without the springboard, but it's very hard to pull that off. Spring-boarding from the high platform won't work because of the ceiling, and it won't work from the other platforms available as they are too far below. A big part of this puzzle is merely realizing that it is a puzzle, and that springboard placement is the key.

Gnarly does more than Vanilla Secret 1, as it should, considering its position in the game, but it also shows the limits of what the designers could do with vertical design. In Vanilla Secret 1, there are climbable vines, springboards of various kinds, and plenty of patrolling Wing Koopas. Gnarly uses plenty of springboards and adds the motorized rope, but it doesn't do a ton with either of those things. The really interesting things all happen in the vines. These four vines contain a puzzle.

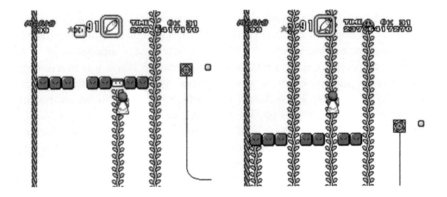

By destroying this block, the second vine can climb significantly higher, leading to an extra life. This is a unique puzzle, but it only uses elements that are already familiar to the player. It's an easy intuitive leap to figure this puzzle out, but only once the player has actually seen the area where the puzzle takes place. There's nothing a player can do to refresh the vines in this level, and so the puzzle is a one-time offer, at least per level. Certainly, the designers could have inserted some kind of reset button unique to this level or offered a pipe loop at the bottom of the level. The first option, though, would involve the designers adding largely superfluous mechanics, which isn't something Nintendo's team did too often in the early 90s. The second option would involve dropping all the way back to the bottom of the level on every puzzle attempt, which is also something that doesn't fit with the design team's style. Essentially, the designers could have done more with the vine puzzle here, but not without changing their game in a larger way, and so they simply obeyed the established borders of their design.

The second puzzle is similar in that it involves a common level design element elaborated in an unusual way. To access the hidden Yoshi Coins for this level, as well as several hidden extra lives, the player has to find a way to ferry this P-Block up to the divider in the level to take advantage of the short timer and enter the otherwise inaccessible pipe.

It's not an easy set of jumps because of the narrow landing and enhanced momentum, but a cape helps. The only real criticism I have of this puzzle is that this is one of the least-known secrets in *Super Mario World* because the P-block is so far away from the part of level it meaningfully modifies. That said, if there is an appropriate place for complicated, atypical puzzles, the Special zone is it. It's not a repeatable lesson that would work in modern games (Google has killed these kinds of puzzles), but it does adhere to the design principles of the game, so it deserves mention.

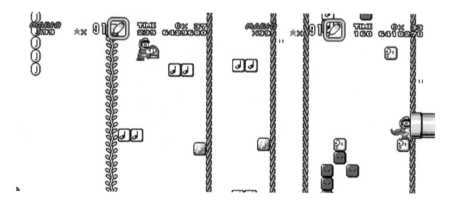

In both cases, the player ends the level by facing off against an enemy in a raised position that hurls intercepts. It's plausible that this is a coincidence, or a product of general principles that the design team was following during the project. My theory, however, is that these levels were intentionally designed alike because one is a direct evolution of the other, along thematic lines.

Irregular Levels: Isolated Concepts

Star World 1

One of the things we've seen several times in this analysis of *Super Mario World* is the technique of rewarding the player with easy fun. Obviously, this is a game, and so the whole thing is supposed to be fun. It's also not a niche game, so the whole thing is supposed to be fairly easy. Ease and fun are both relative concepts here. Star World 1 conveys a sense of what we might call "silliness" in gaming, a feeling that arises out of a minimal amount of danger. Danger is essential to a platformer; that is to say, without some risk, the game isn't a game. Obviously, there can be too much danger so that the playing of the game feels exhausting, especially to new players. Sometimes a really hard level like that is fun, but at other times, it's nice to play a level that's tame and short, and only has enough danger to keep the player's attention.

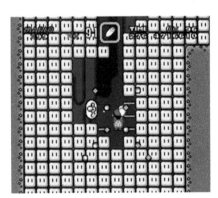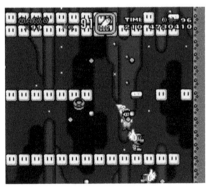

Star World 1 has no bottomless pits. It has few enemies, and all of them are easily avoided. It offers numerous powerups, coins, and the opportunity for extra lives. All of the level is navigated by ridiculously long chains of spin jumps. It's also got the most super stars of any level, and they're all close to one another. It's a kind of bonanza, where the player can indulge several "what-if?" impulses at once.

The artistry in this level isn't merely that it's a silly level with a jackpot of powerups located at the bottom. The artistry is in the level's placement in the game. Nearly a quarter century of exposure (and, more recently, the existence of YouTube) has exposed this game's secrets. Once upon a time, though, a player would have been pretty proud of discovering the Star Road and felt perhaps both relieved and somewhat tired after the effort. This level, with its lighthearted gameplay, makes the perfect denouement to that tension.

Star World 3

Star World 3 does something that seems totally commonplace to players and designers today, but which was actually rather unusual back then. Star World 3 features a one-challenge level. In the age of casual games, online flash arcades and indie niche titles, a one-challenge level is a part of the design vocabulary. It makes sense, too: why not break up levels into obviously discrete chunks which can be digested in small sessions? It also works for skill development via repetition, as it's quick to load and quick to retry.

This level looks exactly like the kind of phenomenon described above, and it operates similarly, too. Here, the player's goal is to get into Lakitu's cloud by knocking him out of it with a kicked block.

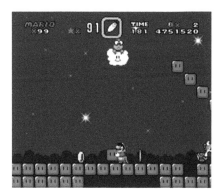 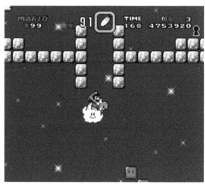

This is a skill that is very specific and rarely used, and therefore perfect for a one-challenge level.

Donut Plains 1

Donut Plains 1 features a number of challenges that do not fit neatly into any of my classifications. There isn't a standard progression of evolutions, expansions, and so on, although the challenges do change across the course of the level. Principally, this is because Donut Plains 1 has more in common with the game's first two levels than it does with any of the rest. The goal of this level is to show the player how to use the cape powerup, and so we see some great tutorial challenges and a steady back-and-forth composite rhythm. The level begins by forcing the player to fly. Leaping to avoid the projectiles from the first Pitching Chuck will lead to this:

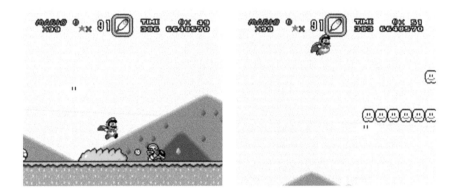

Much like in Yoshi's Island 2, there's a lot of extra space for the player to run through before the next challenge. The difference here is that this space allows Mario to gain enough speed that any jump will cause cape-flight. The Pitching Chuck presents a hazard that requires a jump, and therefore the designers "trick" the player into flight. Naturally, the design team has placed a platform in the sky that confirms the appropriateness of the soaring leap and shows that cape-flights can often be rewarding and fun. The level is filled with extra opportunities to do the same, although the design team doesn't really go out of their way to coerce the player into flight as they do here. This idea also doesn't really develop across the course of the level, which is why this level isn't included in a theme.

The designers spend the rest of the level reinforcing the many other basic skills associated with the cape. For example, the level declines sharply toward action in these two spots, featuring the Volcano Lotus.

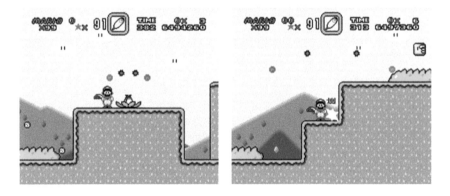

The arc of the Lotus's fireballs precludes all but full-momentum cape-jumps, which aren't easily possible in either location without foreknowledge of the challenge and a concrete plan. What the player is forced into doing is using the lateral cape attack. Attacking with the cape is an essential skill, and once again the designers trick the player into using it.

This level also does a great job of isolating the most common cape-based skill: the gliding descent. Because of the way jumping to max height works (the player has to hold the jump button), cape gliding is very intuitive and will happen before these challenges. Nevertheless, the designers expose the player to challenges that require more nuanced cape glides. The first example is here:

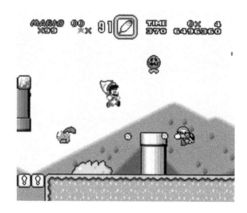

The rapid approach of the Super Koopa will likely force a jump out of the player while Mario is still in stride. The baseballs thrown by the Chuck behind it will necessitate a cape glide, while the Leaping Pumpkin Plant will act as the upward limit of the glide's trajectory. The Pumpkin Plant also necessitates a quick dismount from this pipe and the buildup of some new momentum to outrun the Chuck's baseballs when he turns to track Mario. This is a wonderful introduction to a cape glide technique the player will be using all game. Frequently, and especially in preservation of momentum theme levels, the player will have to glide Mario to a landing spot before immediately taking off into a full-momentum stride, and this level forces the player to do just that without being too difficult. In essence, the designer is "tricking" the player into learning a technique.

There are other examples of the level reinforcing these skills, but they only do just that—reinforce them. While the first two levels of the game do a good job of displaying skills, this level is the best in the game for forcing the player into the precise situations which will expose the use of skills that will last the whole game.

Groovy

Groovy is about the action uses of Yoshi, as directly as any level can be "about" some single idea in this game. To that end, most of the places where a platforming solution would ordinarily be possible, this level offers only an action solution. The principal implement that the designers use to accomplish this emphasis on action, and Yoshi in particular, is the Pokey. The Pokey has thus far only been featured in levels that offer Yoshi within them. Until this point, however, the player hasn't seen any complications that would prevent Mario from simply jumping over the Pokey. In Groovy, challenges involving the Pokey never allow an easy jump; Mario needs momentum to get his feet clear of a five-block height, and even then, if the arc isn't right, he can take damage going up or coming down.

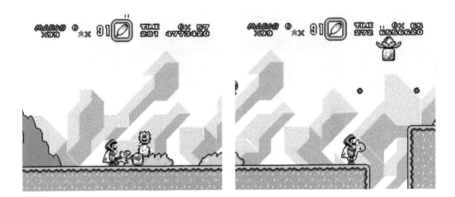

These are the two elements that constitute a standard challenge in this level. Added together, they make it essentially impossible for Mario to get up and over a Pokey safely. Thus, you could call the challenge pictured below and left the standard challenge. Here, the player could conceivably jump to safety, but it's much easier to just use Yoshi's tongue to attack the enemy.

On the right is the expansion/evolution of that challenge, in which the available space is contracted, the geography changes putting Mario at a height disadvantage, and the number of Volcano Lotuses goes up. Combat is necessary not once but twice, as it's still a tough jump with the Pokey gone.

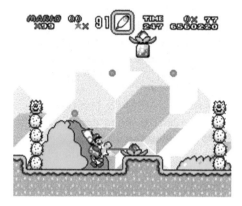

It's much easier to do a small hop and have Yoshi eat the bottom Lotus than to try to jump between them, especially with the Pokey coming from the other side and the fireballs descending from above.

There are several more situations that force action uses of Yoshi. The next one, chronologically, is a different evolution of the standard challenge. This (below, left) is about as obvious as the game gets, in terms of telling the player what he or she needs to do.

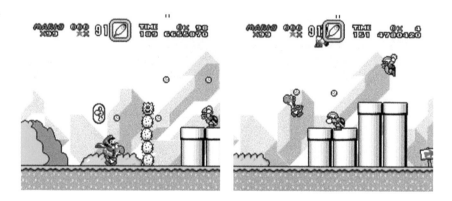

The challenge on the right, meanwhile, is a direct evolution of the double-Lotus challenge from before. This time, the Lotuses evolve into the much more dangerous Pitching Chucks. The need to dispose of that Pokey is just as great as ever, though, as getting over him in a single bound will end in a face-full of deadly, pixelated baseballs.

Interestingly, this is another one of those few levels that actively prevents sustained flight. There are numerous (at least four) walls hidden just above the visible screen that stop Mario's progress if he tries to fly indefinitely over the level.

It seems even the designers realized the biggest flaw in their game, albeit late in the process when they were crafting the weirdest final levels. It makes sense, in the context of this level, that only Yoshi-based combat can get the player through, and all exploits to circumvent this have been eliminated.

The Intros—Yoshi's Island 1 & 2

After much examination, my analysis of the first two levels in the game is that while they display no particularly inspired design ideas, it would have been inappropriate for them to have done so. In *Super Mario Bros. 3*, the first level of the game featured a few powerups and gave the player the opportunity to use a few common mechanics. That level is over before the player has tried even one tenth-of the skills they'll need to know—and the next few levels increase in difficulty pretty quickly. Based on the overall style of *Super Mario World*, all of its carefully delineated skill themes and gradually ascending complexity, it wouldn't make sense to give the player a brief survey before sending them out into harder levels. While the first two levels are boring from the point of view of a design study, that dullness is necessary for a game that wants to make itself accessible to a wide audience.

Yoshi's Island 1 does a good job of introducing a variety of terrain types that will be important in challenges throughout the game. The most obvious terrain type is the 45-degree ramps, which are present right at the beginning and then again a couple of screens later.

Obviously, there are many times when the player will need manage Mario's momentum on ramps, and these help introduce that skill. Similarly, this level does a good job of introducing small and destructible blocks.

 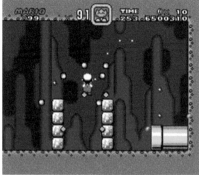

The pipe below the blocks on the left makes it obvious that they're destructible, and their insulated position shows the player how to destroy them (i.e., from above). Meanwhile, the second challenge pictured shows the spinning/jump-through property of these blocks when hit from below—but it also highlights some of the game's physics. Because of the fundamental differences in jumping in *Super Mario World* versus *Super Mario Bros. 3*, landing this jump is an essential exercise in how momentum and jumping mechanics will work for narrow targets.

By way of another example, the mystery coin-block in the sky is an incentive, but the small platforms are a deterrent. Because there are no enemies on this screen, however, the player can take as much time as he or she wants in learning how to land on a one-block platform.

One other unexpected thing in Yoshi's Island 1 leaps out: it features unusual enemies. The Rex, Snapping Chuck, and Banzai Bill are much in the rest of the game, but their presence here seems to make sense for players with no skills. The Banzai Bill is big, but its placement seems to suggest that it's an object lesson in avoiding enemies:

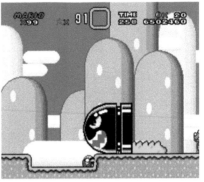

It's easy in each of these cases either to duck or jump to a higher platform. The Chuck and the Rexes make sense in a different way. The Rexes are very similar to Koopas in terms of height and the fact that Mario usually has to jump on them twice to defeat them, but they lack the bouncing shell of a Koopa, which separates the jumping skill from the shell-shooting skill. The Snapping Chuck is also one of the easier varieties of Chuck, especially in this context.

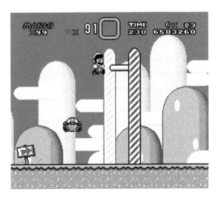

8. The Mini-Theme & Isolated Concepts

One simple enemy-bounce off his head and the player is through the gates and out of danger.

One sweeping truth about both levels is that they're exceptionally wide. That is, not only are they long levels with a ton of time on the level-clock, but they have lots of space between challenges. This is to give the player a cool-down period between events, and probably also to make the player feel like he/she is accomplishing more "game" per challenge solved. It depends how one measures but there are at least eight full screens of space in Yoshi's Island 2 that have no enemies or pitfalls in them.

 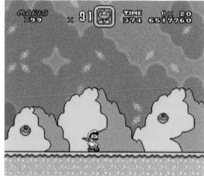

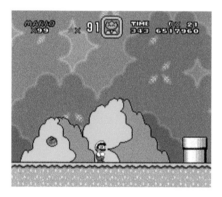

The pitfalls, when they do appear, are neutered in this level; there's never a d-distance of more than two blocks. All this "preparation" distance helps when doing things like encountering the first standard Chuck or the Koopas on the ground. There are plenty of other things introduced, like the Monty Mole and the Piranha vine—but none are as important as Yoshi. Although the Yoshi Fruits never amount to anything important in the game, their use in this level makes a lot of sense. You can see how they encourage the player to jump with a variety of simple trajectories.

The jumps these fruits suggest even include a good approach vector to hitting the Chuck on the head.

These two levels don't do anything very interesting, or even anything particularly clever because they weren't meant to do so. As far as interesting "introductory" levels go, Donut Plains 1 is a fantastic example, although I can't tell if the more intricate things done by that level would have been reasonable if they had come first in the game, before levels like these two.

9

Irregular Levels

Mondo

Mondo is the only level in the game that is neither good nor bad, but rather bewildering from a design perspective. It makes sense that the Special zone would be the place where weird things happen in levels. The player probably won't access the Special zone until deep into the game after mastering lots of skills, and completion of the zone is not mandatory by any means. That said, all of the rest of the levels in the special zone are weird (generally because they are extreme), but they're also basically coherent. Sometimes that coherence is still unfair, but at least it makes some kind of sense. Mondo is both incoherent and unfair, although this unfairness can be exploited.

The baffling element in this level is the variable water level, and in particular, the period of its variability and its directional momentum. The water level will change, from a depth of six above ground level, and then will cycle back in about 35 game-seconds. (The first cycle is different, but the rest are fairly regular.)

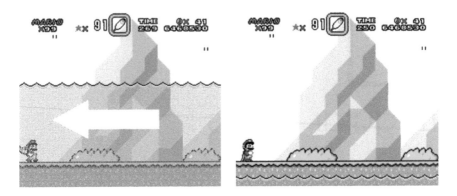

The water does more than institute the normal water physics; this water has a direction. While in the water, Mario's momentum going toward the level's end will be reduced to the speed of underwater walking. This environmental shift in directional momentum can make even the simplest tasks very annoying, as the skills the player has been using all game are now befuddled by an element present in no other level. In this regard, the level has much in common with Tubular.

The reason why this is baffling and not merely bad is the water level is on a timer and not synced to Mario's location. The player will sometimes be forced to deal with a Flying Hammer Brother while Mario is being pushed backwards by the water (an effect the enemies do not experience, naturally). This is unnecessarily difficult, but all the player has to do is wait for the water level to go down and the challenge becomes significantly more reasonable.

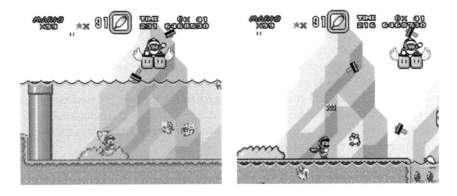

There are obvious problems with waiting 15 seconds. For one thing, it's boring, and being boring is one of the worst crimes a game can commit. For another thing, these extra waiting periods mess up the theoretical timing of the level. If the player continually presses forward without any waiting period, the water sections tend to line up with some architectural features that make it seem like the timing is somehow appropriate. Then there are sections like these that don't make sense in this scheme. Are these sections supposed to be wet or dry?

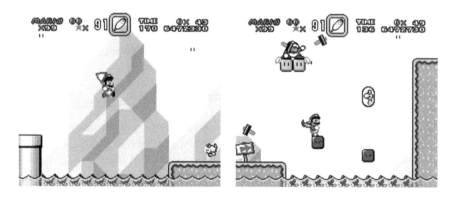

These pits are ten blocks wide, making them the longest pits in the game not mitigated by some powerup or other gravity-defying factor like a balloon, springboard, or pipe-cannon. In essence, this is the kind of challenge perfectly suited for the end of a game. The problem is that the presence of the water makes these jumps somewhat of a non-challenge, or at least a very bizarre one. Why are those two blocks present above the second big pit if the water is supposed to rise? Or is it not supposed to rise at all? The level might have made more sense if the water had been linked to location instead of time, but maybe this was a technological impossibility. Whatever reason they might have had for making the odd decisions they did, the design team rolled out a weird one in this level.

Chocolate Island 5

Although Chocolate Island 5 isn't in the Special zone, I think it probably would have been placed there if the designers had the space. Chocolate Island 5 takes two cadence-unfriendly ideas and makes a whole level out of them. The first idea in play is the P-Switch puzzle, which is stretched out across half a level. This puzzle's trick is convincing the player to hit the switch as soon as Mario stumbles upon it, and to that end the level presents plenty of temptations.

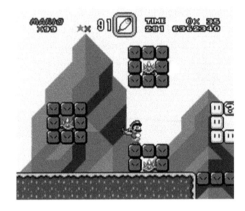

The obvious message is clear: hit a P-Switch and all of this will become available. I like this as a psychological effect because it tricks the player into making a stupid, knee-jerk reaction. Obviously, those empty coin-blocks will transform after the switch is hit, but why would the player want to actually do this? To free all the Spiny enemies inside those blocks? Less obviously, if the player actually thinks about the effect of the switch instead of simply reacting, he or she will notice that the switch either shouldn't be hit or that there might be a better opportunity later, and there is! By bringing the switch toward the roulette block, the player can get a star and possibly a series of 1-ups.

This is where the identification with the Special zone is the clearest from a design perspective. To know exactly what the level expects from the player (ideally, to collect the star and then chain some 1-ups together), the player probably has to have already seen what lies ahead. This would be totally acceptable in a Special zone level because those levels do weird, tricky and extreme things with the design of the game; that's the point of the zone. This is the last level in Chocolate Island, and while it's a nice break from the increasing difficulty of the game, it's out of place.

The second part of the level is also strange. While most of Chocolate Island has been about taking ideas from earlier in the game and expanding and evolving them, this section does something more extreme. This jump, located at the end, is a tough jump.

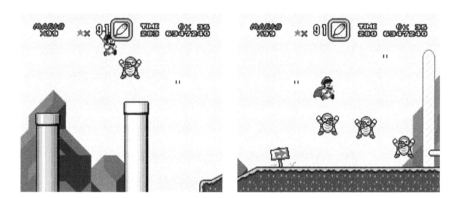

Because the Snapping Chuck is programmed to make its jump only when Mario is in range, the player has to shape Mario's jump arc so that Mario is still four blocks above the pipe (and the Chuck) after he's cleared five blocks of d-distance. It's not an impossible jump, but it is difficult, and the player also has to make sure not to start jumping when the moveable pipe Mario is standing on begins to sink. It seems almost as if it could fit somewhere else more appropriately. And if that weren't enough, there are also these Chucks at the end, which are very reminiscent of the end of Funky. Again, this isn't bad design, it's just out of place in the overall progression of the game.

Funky

The apparent purpose of Funky was to allow the design team to get more use out of some enemies they liked: the Sumo Brother and the Alerting Chuck. Neither enemy sees much action outside this level, but they see plenty of development here. Although the level itself doesn't resemble any of the four central themes, it does exhibit a surprisingly normal cadence. The level begins with a single Sumo Brother for the standard challenge (left) and evolves quickly (right).

The evolution is that now the player can't simply make a timed run through the Sumo Brother's area; Mario has to either make a confined leap over the enemy or defeat him from below.

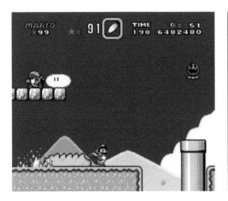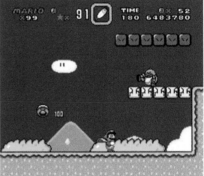

Next, we have an expansion that doubles the number of Sumo Brothers. Ignoring the unusual composition of the blocks (which is a red herring anyway), this is about as standard as an expansion can get.

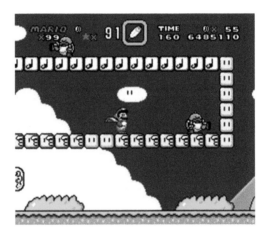

The level has two enemies it wants to feature and so the Alerting Chuck appears next. Although accompanied by a Pitching Chuck, the two are separated by a decent amount of space, and so this is probably best assessed as a second standard challenge for a level with two cadences. We'll see the evolution of this in a bit.

Next, the level goes back to an expansion upon the standard challenge (below, left). Although the Sumo Brother is vulnerable here, he's also a lot closer to the ground, meaning that Mario has less time to dodge the lightning bolt and less space to jump above the fire. The evolution of the Alerting Chuck follows next.

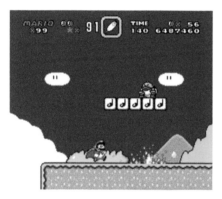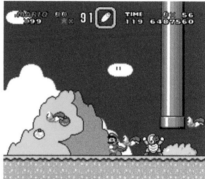

The second Alerting Chuck (on the right, above) is an obvious evolution via the terrain; now the player must hit and defeat the Chuck to pass by because of the confining pipe. Hitting the Chuck from above will alert the Super Koopas, though, and will not only make this challenge more difficult, but the next challenge as well.

There are two really significant challenges left, the first of which is what we might call the "orthodox" pinnacle challenge. This Sumo challenge is complicated by these Wing Goombas (left, below). This is the first time in the level another enemy has been added to a Sumo Brother challenge, and so clinically speaking it's the most complex. It's a weak climax though, and so there's a greater challenge yet to come.

This wall of Chucks has nothing to do with the evolutions we've seen so far, and so although it's outside the cadence, it's still the true culminating challenge of the level.

Vanilla Dome 1

Vanilla Dome 1, much like the level that comes after it, does not exhibit the normal cadence structure we find in most levels. It does feature several sections that would fit easily into a skill theme, but because there's no progression in any thematic direction, the level doesn't belong to any of those themes. The probable "goal" or lesson that this level is supposed to teach the player, is how to deal with narrow corridors and low ceilings, and how those things affect jumps. Precisely controlling the height of Mario's jumps is a very important skill later in the game. Although this level does not, except for one instance, call for a controlled-height jump, it nevertheless prepares the player for their use in several ways. The challenge below seems bizarre in the context of the game's skill themes but makes sense from a perspective of low-height jumps.

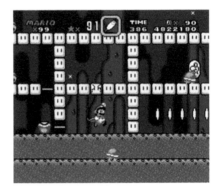

The Buzzy Beetle that moves along the lowest level of this challenge will likely force Mario to jump, landing him in one of the "sealed" boxes. Although there's nothing particularly difficult about this challenge, it does put the player's mind on the fact that some jumps can be too high, and that it's important to note what's above Mario as well as in front or below of him. The second section teaches a similar lesson through different means. This section features a Super Star and a sinking platform. Like all sinking platforms and almost all stars, this is the mark of a preservation of momentum challenge, but the lesson the player needs to learn here isn't about that theme, it's about controlling the height of Mario's jumps.

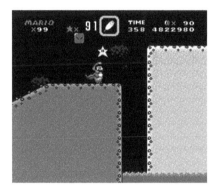 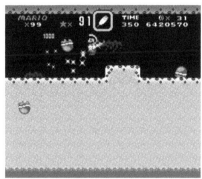

The raised hump in the terrain forces Mario, who must be running at full speed, to jump. Yet, in order to hit all of the enemies to get the 1-up, Mario's arc can't take him too far. By limiting the height of the jump—and there are several ways to do this—Mario can not only survive the platform but also get the 1-up via the star.

The last section features some Spike Tops that continue to highlight the perils of low-ceilinged corridors. Although this whole level is somewhat atypical for the game, this section in particular is weird in that these enemies move so slowly.

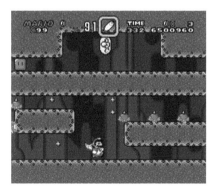 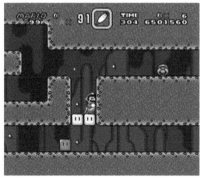

The corridors that follow are similarly dull and repeat the same low-ceiling idea again without any interesting ideas. If there is a filler level, or even a filler section of the game, it seems that this was it.

Tubular

The reason that Tubular is so infamous is not that it is merely difficult, but that it is difficult in a way that does not fit with the style of the game. Tubular has a combination of systemic and local problems that make it unique in *Super Mario World*, and so it feels wrong. *Super Mario World* has few systemic problems, and the ones that exist favor the player. The ability for sustained flight via the cape or Blue Yoshi is a game-breaking systemic problem, but they make the game easier, not harder. Moreover, the player could always forego their use for the sake of enjoying all the ground-based content of the game. There are many local problems throughout the game too, and this text has highlighted many of them, but nowhere do the local problems compound more than in this level.

In Tubular, the systemic problem is that balloon powerup is badly implemented. The powerup isn't a great idea to begin with; it's so dissimilar from everything else in the game that it can't help but feel awkward. Wet and dry levels use vectors differently, but nevertheless are very similar to one another. The balloon powerup changes too many things.

(Green arrows indicate a controllable vector. Yellow arrows indicate a fixed-speed vector. The red arrow is for a polarized vector—one that actively fights the player.)

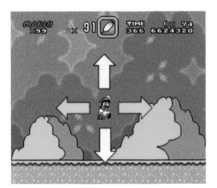 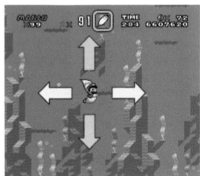

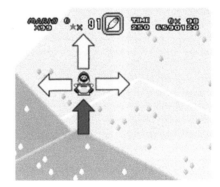

This illustration shows how wet and dry levels are really not that different. The biggest change from dry to wet levels is in downward acceleration, but as you can see the full force of this effect isn't felt except in the few situations where Mario drops a full-screen length, and the player can interrupt it with ease. Mario's ability to move laterally is slowed in water levels, but his greater ability to control his vertical position makes up for this, at least to some degree. The balloon powerup, meanwhile, limits Mario's movement even further and in stranger ways. Inverting the effect of the downward pull of the "gravity" of the game isn't a bad idea per se, but matched with all of the other effects, it's too much.

Why did the designers think that it was a good idea to severely limit Mario's ability to move downwards in addition to slowing his lateral movement and even his upwards momentum? Why did they want to eliminate Mario's ability to accelerate completely? These things sound terrible in theory, and in practice they weren't much better. There are some places where this works passably. In Donut Secret 1, there is a bonus pipe-section that gives the player a balloon powerup to ascend to the top of a tall cavern. On the way up, there are a few patrolling Wing Koopas to make navigation interesting, but they're not dense. Because the player never has to go anywhere but up, the speed penalty on downward movement isn't an issue. Because the Koopas aren't dense or speedy, the lateral slowness isn't a huge problem either.

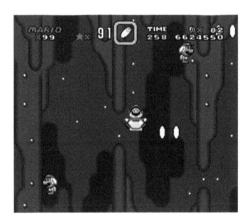

There's also a platform there that Mario can land on before getting the second balloon to ascend the rest of the way. This forms the longest balloon-based challenge in the game (not counting Tubular), and the only one to involve more than one balloon in sequence. Besides the fact that this challenge is built around the movement penalties, it's also over a non-fatal fall. If Mario loses the balloon, he can still land safely. In other words, most of the problems with the balloon are mitigated by level design. The same is true in Donut Secret 2, in which there are intercepts and some dangerous d-distances, but also a safety net.

Falling here is not necessarily fatal, but what's more important is that this challenge is only one P-balloon long. But let's back up to Donut Secret 1 again: when Mario has to get a second balloon in that level, he gets to stand on a platform to do it. Likewise, this section in Forest of Illusion 1 is so short that it too trivializes the problems the balloon has.

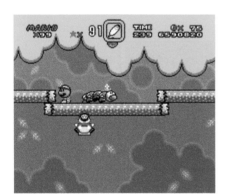 

There's no evolution over the course of these three levels that might prepare the player for Tubular, just a sudden, sharp spike when the player reaches it. Those are just the systemic, game-long problems.

The local problems begin about as soon as the player collects the P-Balloon powerup. One of the bizarre properties of the P-Balloon is that it comes closer to real-world physics in its applications than any other powerup. When the player has to use the springboard to launch Mario toward the balloon, there's an unfortunate drop in altitude.

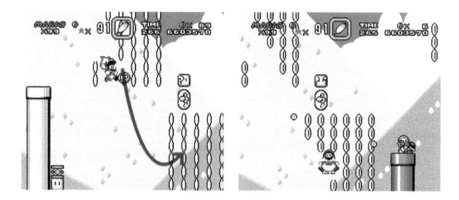

For whatever reason, the inherent lift of the balloon powerup slowly depletes Mario's downward motion instead of stopping it suddenly. This is closer to real-world physics than any interaction involving the cape or Yoshi wings or even the underwater physics. Apart from this break from previously established game-physics, the arc of this jump takes Mario immediately into danger, and does it in a way that the game usually wouldn't do. The two Pitching Chucks here would be tricky if Mario had full use of the ground, but with a balloon they're significantly harder because Mario's lateral movement is restricted, and there's no upward acceleration at all. The only really effective way to avoid this instant-death problem is to know beforehand that the Chucks are waiting off-screen and anticipate the baseballs before they start flying.

This is just the tip of the iceberg, so to speak because this challenge evolves and expands. The first evolution is an A + B evolution, which adds a group of Wing Koopas to the projectile challenge the player has just faced.

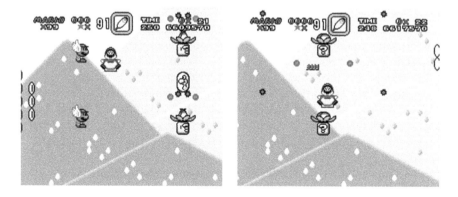

The projectile portion of the challenge has mutated, going from lateral baseballs to vertical fireballs, but it's still limited to a small portion of the screen, which is an important detail—it's still a challenge that the player can figure out on the fly. Adding the Wing Koopas means that a first-time player has to shoot the gaps between them and the Volcano Lotuses at once, which can be difficult, but at least the entire challenge is visible to the player at once.

The third challenge is the real disaster area, and the point at which the last of the systemic problems with the P-Balloon appears and combines with its biggest local problem. This challenge is probably supposed to be a mutation or slight evolution of the first balloon challenge, and if it weren't for the confounding problems with the powerup itself, it might not be much harder. As it stands, though, the whole thing is poorly conceived.

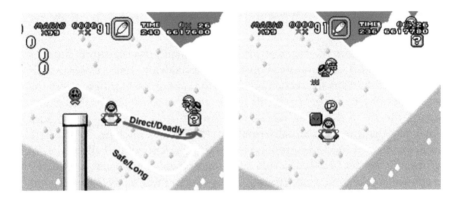

The path in the third challenge (left) is a problem because the Pumpkin pipe forces the player to descend not only downward, but at an angle. In the previous two challenges, the player could easily move in a straight line with proper timing or a couple of quick pauses, which made it easier to intuit the timing for both challenges. Here, the player needs to move Mario downwards and to the right at the same time, or else Mario won't get the next balloon before falling. Then, these Kicking Chucks are calibrated so that they will hit Mario if the player guides him on the shortest path. Ergo, the player has to take Mario through a very specific path, one that is impossible to know before trying and failing the challenge several times.

This brings us to the overall "anti-theme" problem: this level violates most of what makes *Super Mario World* what it is. Part of what made composite design so successful was that it helps designers flesh out the length and depth of their games without forcing players to fail dozens of times in the same spot in order to memorize and precisely execute the exact maneuvers necessary for survival. *Super Mario World* goes further than merely not forcing the player to repeat the same task over and over—it actively prepares players for future challenges by use of skill themes. The ultimate experience of a Mario game is the moment in which the player sees a brand new, harder-than-ever challenge and nails it in one attempt because the skill themes have prepared his/her mind and thumbs for the moment so well. That experience of game-defining flow is the height of artistry in game design. Tubular, especially in this third challenge, is the opposite of that.

Valley of Bowser 1

Although Valley of Bowser 1 does not belong in any particular theme, it does demonstrate several trends that illustrate the increase in qualitative complexity throughout the game. One of the first problems with trying to analyze this game was that the nuts-and-bolts numerical details didn't suggest a way that the game became progressively harder. Jumps don't keep getting wider or higher or more filled with intercepts—or at least not after the halfway point of the game. Analysis of the skill themes shows, however, that the levels do change; Valley of Bowser 1 encapsulates the kind of changes that happen. The level itself strongly recalls Vanilla Dome 1 and 2, as it focuses on low-ceiling combat and maze-like features. Those things, because they are so scarce and so generally out of line with the style of the rest of the game, are not terribly interesting. What happens in the tunnels is of more import.

The most obvious level-to-level evolution is the presence of the Mega-Mole in a situation that actually means something. The Mega-Mole appears in Chocolate Island 4 and is completely forgettable. In that level, the Mole was a mere novelty thrown in to make an otherwise enemy-less level more energetic; it did not succeed especially well. That is not the case in Valley of Bowser 1, where there are some real problems that require unusual solutions.

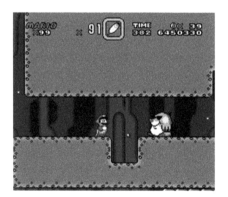 

The player can backtrack, use the cape attack, or Yoshi's tongue. Even though those are three solutions, the room for improvisation and choice is cut down; the corridor is that narrow. It's also clear that there's enough variety in these challenges that they might form a cadence—except that they're not in linear sequence. To see every Monty Mole, the player would have to go through branching, parallel paths in the level, and since backtracking is abnormal for this game, that's probably not what the designers intended.

This level might have made an interesting one if the designers had elected to shift back and forth between the Mega Mole and the Charging Chuck. Certainly, the Chuck challenges are a little more in line with the standard ideas of cadence progression.

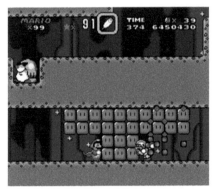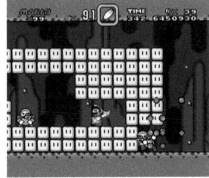

Here, the player needs to manipulate the Chucks into breaking blocks to clear paths, and each challenge is different. The left-hand challenge is too long and needs to be shortened by Mario a bit before the Chuck can be baited into saving the player some time. The right-hand challenge pictured is a great evolution of this, but the player might not encounter this challenge at all. The overall trend for the game—using Chucks as puzzle pieces in dangerous situations—is definitely a qualitative step up.

While this level has little to teach us about the design of *Super Mario World* levels, it has a lot to teach us about the game. The game gets harder when things become more complex. Sometimes this has to do with things that change quantitatively (such as the expansion-by-contraction of those narrow hallways), but it's much more often a change in qualitative complexity. The levels in *Super Mario World* evolve just as challenges in those levels do.

Vanilla Dome 2

Vanilla Dome 2 serves an example of why this book does not examine the design of secret exits in *Super Mario World*. Generally, secret entrances and exits are simply stationed somewhere along the linear path of a level, in places that the player might be unable to access at first, or which the player simply might not notice. There is no meaningful pattern in the secrets, and especially none in those levels which do not hide their secrets in any special way. In levels like Vanilla Dome 2, however, the designers went to greater lengths to involve the secret exit in the level's larger design. In essence, they created a maze, which is great for secrets but bad for consistent level design. Maze sections are few in *Super Mario World*, and if Vanilla Dome 2 is any indication, it's because mazes disrupt the style of the game.

The properties of a real maze seem to be antithetical to skill themes, at least in the way that *Super Mario World* constructs mazes and skill themes. The kind of coherence needed by a simple maze and the kind of coherence that makes a skill theme are not the same. The sections of a maze need to be distinguishable from one another. This is probably why this level has both dry and wet sections.

 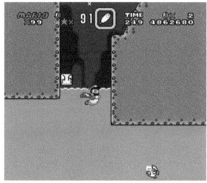

The alternating wet and dry sections help the player to remember and distinguish where various paths and turns were located, and which ones the player has visited (and not visited). If the level had been all wet or all dry, the twists of the mazes might have been indistinct in the player's mind. Additionally, the alternating sections and gimmicky tricks (Chucks plowing through spin-blocks) in the level keep the player on guard.

The problem is that this kind of variety doesn't carry a theme well. Some levels have two standard challenges and are able to develop both. This level has more "standard" challenges than that, and doesn't really develop any of them. The fish movement patterns suggest the periodic enemies theme. The uneven terrain and Beetles foreshadow some of the preservation of momentum challenges from Valley of Bowser. The Chucks and Swoopers later in the level are clearly pieces of intercept challenges.

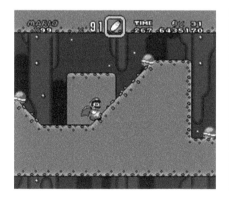 

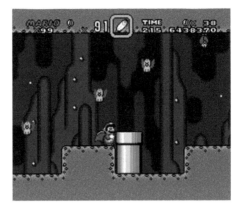

None of these challenges go anywhere because it probably would be too taxing to expect the player to navigate a maze (even a simple one) while dealing with escalating challenges. These challenges are great, however, in giving the player cues about Mario's relative position in the level. Although not an evolution or expansion upon an earlier idea, the large number of enemies pictured on the far right tells the player clearly that Mario has left the maze.

The Toolkit for Cadence Analysis

This chapter looks at two different ways to analyze cadences in *Super Mario World*. Although the levels of *Super Mario World* were probably not designed with them in mind, the designers nevertheless produced patterns that we can benefit from studying and emulating. The reason I'm going to offer two different ways of looking at cadences is because they contain a great deal of useful information. For example, we can understand a lot about *Super Mario World* and its design philosophy by analyzing the whole game statistically. As such, the first section of this chapter looks at statistical data on the balance of evolutions versus expansions, how far apart related challenges are in a cadence, and what those things can tell us about the game as a whole.

The Cadence Chart and Statistical Analysis

There are 67 normal levels in *Super Mario World*; this excludes the Switch Palaces, Top Secret Area, and Bowser's Castle, as they all do things very differently from the rest of the game. Of those 67 normal levels, about 50 of them feature a cadence. (I say "about" because there are some edge cases that could go either way.) Valley of Bowser 2 and Way Cool are good examples of this. In Valley of Bowser 2, there is some semblance of evolutionary progression, but it's not strictly linear and doesn't develop very much. Similarly, in Way Cool, it's hard to know which of the multiple paths would constitute the cadence. One might make any number of cadences out of Way Cool, or that might defeat the point. A related problem crops up when analyzing the ghost houses; their circuitous paths and puzzles are interesting the first time through, but rarely make for a real cadence. There are definitely some evolutions and expansions (found in Forest Ghost House, in particular), but they rarely exhibit the structure that is so clear in the other levels. For those 50-or-so levels, there are some interesting underlying statistics we can pull out. But how do we do that?

One way of looking at those levels is to put them into a two-line *cadence chart*. I gave a brief example of this in the introduction and in Chapter 3, but I'll recapitulate that again here in a little more detail. The top line of the chart tells us which challenge we're examining. The bottom line tells us which challenge the current challenge modifies.

$$
\begin{array}{c|c|c|c|c|}
\mathbf{S} & \mathbf{1} & \mathbf{2} & \mathbf{3} & \\
\hline
& \mathbf{V{:}S} & \mathbf{X{:}1} & \mathbf{V{:}S} &
\end{array}
$$

The standard challenge doesn't modify any previous challenge. The first iteration evolves the standard challenge. Iteration two expands the evolution. (This pattern of "standard, evolution, expansion" is the most common way that the designers begin a cadence in *Super Mario World*, by the way. If you're going for that "Nintendo feel," you might lead with this pattern). Iteration three evolves the standard in a new way.

There are a bunch of useful things that charts like this can do. For one thing, we can figure out the proportions of evolutions and expansions in a level, a section of a level, or an entire game. The graph below charts the results of each analyzed cadence, but it requires some explanation as well.

PROPORTIONS OF CHALLENGE TYPES IN *SMW* CADENCES

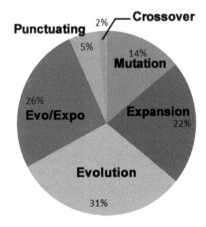

The most important thing is that evolution challenges are the most frequent type in a *Super Mario World* cadence. This fits right in with the notion that qualitative changes are more important for this game than quantitative ones, even in the short term. Qualitative changes (evolution and mutation) to challenges make up nearly half the game's content. Another large portion is made up of challenges that are both evolutions and expansions. On balance, qualitative changes are slightly more important than quantitative ones. This doesn't diminish the role of expansion challenges, which are still necessary, but it does show the where the game gets its flavor. The second biggest thing to note is that there are more crossovers than were counted in the graph; the problem is in classification. Throughout the game there were many instances in which a crossover element (usually from the complementary theme) is added to a challenge to make it into an evolution challenge. The most important information about any one of those challenges is that it is an evolution because this will be relevant to every other challenge that follows. For example, Larry's Castle is definitely in the moving targets theme, as most of the level is conducted around a moving platform.

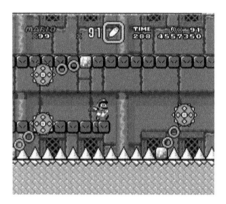 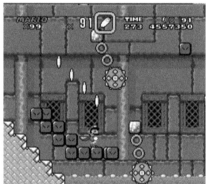

This level, however, has an enormous amount of periodic enemies, so there are crossover challenges all over the place. They aren't counted as "pure" crossovers in this statistical analysis. It's more important to see how they're evolving, expanding, and mutating within the framework of that level and the moving targets theme. The crossover challenges recorded in the graph are only the "pure" crossovers, such as the one found at the mid-gate in Vanilla Dome 3.

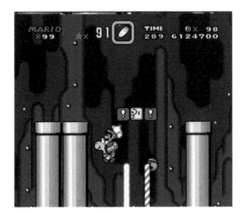

This is a pure crossover to the complementary theme, with no moving platforms in sight. Obviously, it's very short, but that's what I mean by "pure" crossovers.

Punctuating challenges, on the other hand, are genuinely few. The designers of *Super Mario World* were quite fastidious about making sure that their cadences were really coherent. I submit, however, that this means a lot. When we play Super Mario levels, we hardly ever think "oh, not another one of these" about any given challenge in a level. (Well, maybe sometimes, but not often). Yet, if this pattern holds true for most Mario games, then it means that levels actually don't need much variety, if they're not too long. One or two ideas are more than enough to fill a level if those ideas are evolved, expanded, and mutated in the right ways.

This brings up a very big question, though: what are these "right ways" to evolve, mutate, and expand? We're actually going to spend most of the rest of this section looking at how statistics about the cadences give us some answers to that question. The first thing to look at is a more advanced breakdown of statistics across the skill themes.

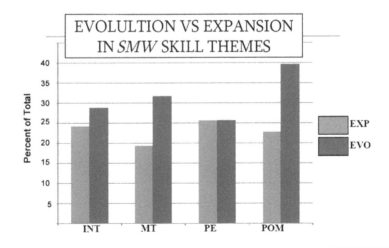

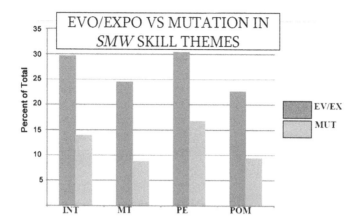

EVO/EXPO VS MUTATION IN *SMW* SKILL THEMES

These two graphs say a lot. This is a statistical breakdown of the challenge types by skill theme. The first graph confirms the designers' general bias towards the evolution challenge—except in the periodic enemies theme. There are a few more interesting points, however. First, the action themes feature a greater proportion of expansion events than do their platform counterparts. They also see more mutation. I think this is attributable to the nature of the action declension. It is easier for designers to simply add more intercepts or periodic enemies to a level than it is to add more moving platforms. In fact, it seems from the design of the levels examined earlier in this book that these expansions had to happen in order for the action themes to develop. Frequently, those intercepts and periodic enemies evolve from a Koopa to a Chuck, or from a fireball to a smashing pillar. The designers of *Super Mario World* kept the number of different kinds of enemies in any single level pretty low, and so those evolutionary substitutions can only take a level so far. Expansions need to fill in the rest of the level's content. Interestingly, Mutations are more common in the action-declension themes for the same reason. When evolutions and expansions can't go any further, mutations fill the void. Evolution/expansion combo challenges, meanwhile, are basically the same as the incidence of expansion and evolution challenges generally; action themes have more of them because they have more expansions.

Platforming-declension levels, despite having a lesser degree of parity between their evolution and expansion challenges, don't seem to suffer for it. The obvious explanation for their relative lack of expansions is that the designers saw that d-distances and delta-heights either couldn't or just didn't need to go up across the course of the game. Whether this design strategy is universal for platformers or whether other platformers do more with expansions remains to be seen. I would certainly love to write a book on the subject, but this information does tell us a lot about the average composition of a cadence both in the game of *Super Mario World* and in its individual themes.

There are a few other details that the chart method can provide us with. The chart I've used so far is just a static image, but cadence charts can also be viewed and processed in a spreadsheet.

A	B	C	D	E	F	G	H	I	J	K
C5	MOD	TYPE	DECLENSION	M ELEMENT	C6	MOD	TYPE	DECLENSION	M ELEMENT	C7
V	1	ADDITION	ACTION	INTERCEPT	X	5	A+B	ACTION	COMBO OF PREV	VX

This chart includes counters, types of evolutions, information about genre elements and could include much more. I want to focus on the few details that I used the most. The details in question are challenge type, the challenge the current one modifies, and the distance between the parent challenge and child challenge. (If challenge B evolves challenge A, then I call A the parent and B the child.)

LEVEL	THEME	MIDGATE	C2	MOD	DIST	C3	MOD	DIST	C4	MOD	DIST	C5	MOD	DIST	C6	MO
VOB4	INT	3	VX	1	1	M	2	1	X	1	3	V	4	1	V	
BABB1	MT		V	1	1	VX	1	1	X	2	2	M	1	4	VX	

The MOD and DIST statistics are very simple. Every challenge in a cadence modifies some previous challenge. For example, you can see some challenges from Valley Fortress just below.

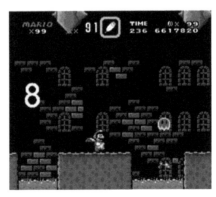

Challenge four in Valley Fortress modifies challenge three by expanding the d-distance of the spike pits. Challenge five expands the number of pylon/island combos in challenge four to three. Then, in the second half of the level, challenge eight is actually modifying challenge three, too! It goes all the way back and starts a different branch of expansion and evolution. That's why the DIST figure for the new branch would be five because it expands and evolves a jump event from five challenges ago.

I like these three stats as they give us mathematical backing for the cadence shapes we're going to look at in the next section. That is to say, big jumps in DIST help to reveal major level branches—especially when those jumps are followed by further development. For example, if you're charting a cadence and you see that the DIST figure for various evolutions starts to get bigger and bigger, you're looking at a theme and variation cadence. If you're looking at a level and there's only one big DIST jump, you're probably looking at a fork cadence or a bow cadence. If there are no large DIST figures at all, you might be looking at a stem cadence. If the DIST figure is almost always two or three, that's a good indication you're looking at a trill cadence. We're going to visualize all of those cadences in the next section, but I wanted to explain the value of cadence charts in identifying cadence shapes.

The Visual Cadence Map

The goal of this type of cadence analysis is to visualize the high-level structures at work in a level's cadence. The designers of *Super Mario World* repeated themselves (probably without meaning to) in the way they laid out many of their levels. By visualizing the way that evolutions and expansion relate to one another, and relate back to the standard challenge, we can understand the repeated structures and design strategies at work in this game. The concepts behind this analysis are a little tricky at first, but the process of making a cadence map is simple. The first step is to simply plot the standard challenge.

From there, we simply have to draw in the connections between iterations.

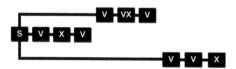

As before, the X and V signify evolutions and expansions (and XV signifies that one challenge does both), while M signifies a mutation. Because the lines between challenges signify the connections, we don't have to use any enumeration as we might in a cadence chart.

I want to state here that for these diagrams, the y-and x-axes can be deceptive. The only hard-and-fast rule about this type of diagram is that distance along the x-axis correlates exactly with progress through a level. It does not necessarily mean that those challenges are more complex. The y-axis, meanwhile, does not scale in any linear way. In this example, I use the y-axis to separate family relationships between challenges. I feel that this information is the most widely applicable. That is to say, if you wanted to take the cadence of your favorite *Super Mario World* level and transpose it onto another game engine, this tool would help you to do that. It would not, however, account for difficulty. I do not believe it is possible to directly translate the difficulty of one game to another—only the general structure.

Given all of that, how and when do branches form? Every time there is an evolution that adds a new element that sees continued iteration, it creates a new branch of the family. That branch gets a fixed position on the y-axis. This doesn't mean that every evolution creates a new branch. Some evolutions add something new, but that idea doesn't receive any independent development. Let's take a look at a level that *does* have separate branches: Chocolate Fortress. (Note that this image is necessarily small to organize all the relevant information in one place. You can see the writeup of this level in Chapter 6 to get a bigger and clearer look at how it works.)

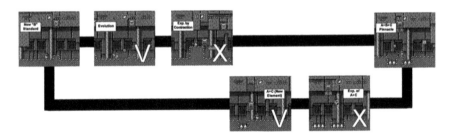

The clearest sign that there are two different branches is that each branch has an expansion of *just that branch's* evolution. That's exactly what you see above. The initial branch gets an expansion, then the alternate branch gets an expansion, and then they merge at the end.

On the other hand, the example below (from Soda Lake) is an example of rearranging elements already introduced to the player without any orthogonal development. For visualization purposes, I don't visualize the evolutions as starting extended branches of the level. Rather, I visualize the evolutions as stubs sticking off the main stem of the expansions.

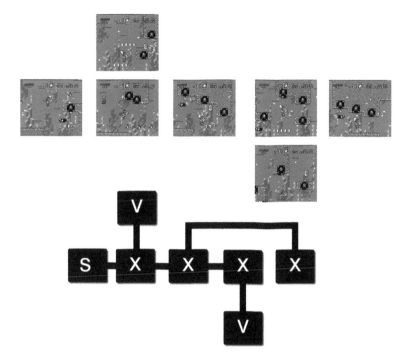

Those evolutions don't really go anywhere; they lack direction. They branch off from one of the expansions, but because they never really develop into anything, their y-axis position isn't terribly significant. The only important thing to know is that they're not part of the main stem of expansions that form the basis of the level. I could probably display them more accurately by doing this.

Because each evolution represents a branch that doesn't go anywhere, they probably would not get their own separate spot on the y-axis. I felt that putting the entire line on the same place on the y-axis would obscure the main stem of the expansions. The purpose of the tool is to extract information, not to obscure it. With all of that in mind, let's take a look at some common cadence shapes from *Super Mario World*.

Cadence Shapes

The Fork Cadence

The first shape I want to highlight is the fork cadence. In this cadence, a level has two primary branches. Usually, at about the halfway point in the level, the designer stops iterating the first set of evolutions, and starts a new branch. For example, this is the cadence of Donut Plains 3.

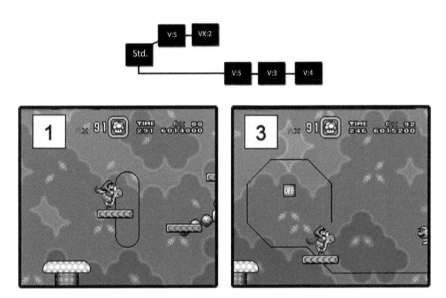

The fork occurs in the third iteration when the level switches from looping platforms to linear platforms. Other good examples of the fork cadence include:

1. Cheese Bridge: The level forks at the changeover from platforms to motorized ropes.
2. Vanilla Dome 4: The level forks when bullets start coming perpendicular as well as parallel to the platforms, around the halfway point.
3. Butter Bridge 2: The level forks around the midgate, when Koopas stop kicking shells from above and the delta height of jumps goes up (because of parallel platforms at different heights).

You should know, however, that not every level that does two things is a fork cadence level. One key sign of a fork cadence is that the central mechanic is preserved, not just the theme. In Donut Plains 3, both sections take place on a moving platform. The same is true of Cheese Bridge. In Butter Bridge 2, the main enemy is always a Super Koopa that swoops down at Mario when he's jumping. That mechanic is maintained across both the flat section with Koopa shells, and the second section with no shells but platforms of varying heights. A level like Chocolate Fortress is not a fork cadence. When that level switches from sharpened logs to Thwomps, it starts a second cadence.

The Bow Cadence

The bow cadence is a lot like the fork cadence, in that there are clear branches in the level. In this case, however, the branches reconnect at the end, bringing all the elements of the level together in one or two final challenges. The best example of this is Chocolate Fortress. We've already seen what the level looks like, but I'll bring it back again here with a pure cadence map.

When the A, B, and C evolutions all come together in the final challenge, the cadence map forms a "bow" (as in "bow and arrow") shape. Other levels that use a bow cadence include:

1. **Outrageous:** This level actually does a lot of crazy things, including having one cadence inside another, but the two cadences come together at the end!
2. **Larry's Castle:** The second half combines Magikoopa, sharpened logs and fireballs in the last challenge. It's actually a little short to be called a full cadence pattern, but it has the structure.

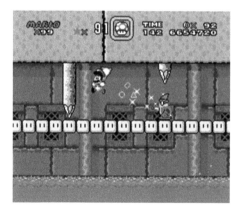

One good identifying tip for the bow cadence: in addition to having elements A, B, and C, it must have A+B, A+C, and A+B+C. Otherwise, you're probably looking at a fork cadence.

The Theme and Variation Cadence

A theme and variation cadence consists of a standard challenge that is reinterpreted by numerous evolutions. This cadence shape can almost look radial because so many of its challenges connect directly back to the standard.

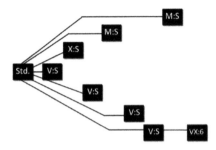

Sometimes, these levels can be easy and fun, and are great for beginners. That said, the level of challenge can still be quite high if the standard challenge is already a tricky one. Levels that have a theme and variation cadence include:

1. Butter Bridge 1
2. Valley of Bowser 4
3. Ludwig's Castle

Although these levels may have expansions in them, they tend to be very evolution-focused to increase the overall variety of ideas.

The Stem Cadence

The stem cadence, which we already looked at briefly in the beginning of this section, is almost the opposite of the theme and variation cadence. In a stem cadence, one idea dominates the level, and every iteration is some kind of direct expansion or evolution of that idea. New ideas may be introduced, but they don't receive expansion or direct iteration.

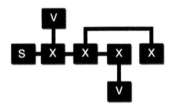

Levels that use the stem cadence include

1. Soda Lake
2. First half of Forest Fortress
3. Forest of Illusion 3
4. Yoshi's Island 4

Stem cadences tend to be heavy on expansions. If one mechanic expands across the level numerous times with little change, you're probably looking at a stem cadence.

Cadence Analysis in the Future

Cadence analysis is a tool, not a dogma. Therefore, I both expect and even hope that other designers and researchers can find new ways to use it. In my mind, the most important thing to know about a cadence is its general shape. Cadence shapes can be carried over from one game to another with relative ease. Difficulty curves are not as easy to move between games. Thus, my favorite method of cadence analysis is a visual map, with evolutionary branches sorted into y-axis positions. That said, time and further research will certainly reveal much more about the study of level design, and the many levels of patterns which exist in this game, and others like it.

Conclusion

The first two things that ought to be addressed in the conclusion are two nagging questions that may have crept into the minds of many readers. The first question is "Does this apply to anything other than Nintendo platformers?" The answer to that is a resounding yes. It doesn't apply to all games, but even a cursory glance into other games will reveal the prevalence of this system. *Donkey Kong Country* levels display clear cadence patterns. *Half-Life* also displays those patterns, although it does so in an idiosyncratic way. (The next entry in this series is on *Half-Life*, if you want to know more). *Mega Man*, *Prince of Persia*, and *Castlevania* all show some of the same design techniques that this game uses. Looking at those games through the same lens of challenge, cadence, and theme would probably have very different results than what we see in this book, but the tools are still up to the task.

The second question is, "Does this system apply to modern 3D games?" The answer is yes, although again, it's definitely not true for all games. An observation struck me during the writing of this book that I think shows that the pattern of challenges, cadences, and skill themes works for more than just 2D titles. After writing the majority of this book, I had the chance to play a number of 3D Mario titles again. It struck me that Mario 64 has not aged very well, whereas the first *Mario Galaxy* is just as replayable today as it was when it came out. Of course,

11 years separate those two titles. In fact, the same amount of time passed between *Super Mario 64* and *Super Mario Galaxy*, as did between the original *Super Mario Bros.* and *Super Mario 64*. That difference is meaningful, but not in the way one might first assume. The great weakness of *Super Mario 64* was one of organization. The big, open, and awkwardly-shaped levels can be confusing even to players who once beat the game. Having seven overlapping objectives strewn across an irregular, open level is no way to construct a coherent game—as the camera clearly shows! Certainly, some of the Lakitu-cam's dreadful mechanics were a result of Nintendo's inexperience in 3D. It's not like there were many 3D games whose example they could have followed. Much of the camera's bad behavior can be blamed on the level design, too. Programming a camera that can follow Mario through the weird, experimental architecture of those levels would be a truly onerous task. *Super Mario Sunshine*, which used a very similar design scheme, did a little bit better with its camera but it still has a reputation for having levels that are hard to see.

Super Mario Galaxy solves many of the problems with level organization and camera problems by changing its design. The purpose of the "galaxy" formation is to create discrete challenges in a 3D environment. Any time the designers can use discrete challenges, evolutions, expansions, and mutations suddenly become very useful and easy to execute. Yes, there are still some larger, open sections of levels that have wonky camera movements. In essence, *Super Mario Galaxy* manages to reclaim the best design aspects of the 2D Mario games and reiterate them in a 3D game. Even as technology and tastes have changed, the best organization practices still apply.

With all of that in mind, here are a few brief lessons we can take away from *Super Mario World*.

Standardize Your Sizes and Distances

It is immensely helpful to both the player and the designer for every size and distance in the game to be divisible into obvious, standardized increments. *Super Mario World* does this by measuring everything in whole coin-block-lengths. Because all platforms, distances, and obstacles correspond to the coin-block size, it's much easier for the player to intuit how difficult any given jump event should be, at least as far as the size of the jump affects that difficulty. It's also easier for the designer to calculate and modify a jump by increasing or reducing it by a block length. This reliance on unambiguous whole-block lengths avoids one of the greatest flaws in a platformer, which when a player asks in frustration, "Am I supposed to be able to make that jump?" Recently, I played through the original *Donkey Kong Country*, and found myself asking that question quite a bit, even as I got deeper into the game. For various technological and/or aesthetic reasons, there are many points in the game where the terrain is structured so that it's unclear whether a given jump is possible, or at what spot the player is supposed to start a jump. This ambiguity is problematic. It's hard to know whether a player is failing in these situations because he or she is messing up the jump or whether the jump isn't supposed to be possible at all.

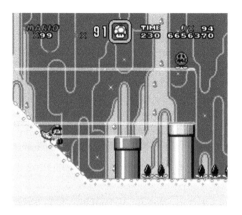

Slopes like these in *Super Mario World* are the closest the game comes to truly ambiguous distances. The slope in Donut Secret 2 slides through block lengths, but there's still no ambiguity because the player can figure out the sizes of things from landmarks on either side of the slope. From this clearly measured context, the player can intuit the plausibility of any given jump, and then deduce if there's a missed path or some required technique not immediately apparent. Trial and error may still be necessary, but at least the clues are there. What's more, it's not as though the designers had to go through and make sure every slope was surrounded by an obvious context; standardization of sizes takes care of all of that naturally.

Some extra guidelines:

- *Super Mario World* standardizes height and width to the same measure, which is one coin-block length. Standardizing to two different units of height and width might have unforeseen complications, but we know the strengths of one standard.
- The standard unit must be large enough to be intelligible. Players aren't going to be using a ruler on every jump, but they will internalize the size of jumps if the unit is large enough that the difference between a jumpable obstacle and a non-jumpable obstacle is clear. One thing that *Super Mario World* does is it makes the standard unit of measure for the game the same width as the player character. It's easy enough for a player to quickly estimate the size of a jump by the size of their character.

Don't Use Real Physics, Especially Not Real Gravity

Real physics are complex. Consider that we pay millions of dollars to professional athletes who make it their business to manipulate the physics of their own bodies to score points, in one way or another. Yes, those athletes are also in incredible physical condition, and they work hard to become so. A videogame can grant you an approximation of a professional athlete's abilities, but there is no controller in the world sophisticated enough to grant you accurate control over a well-trained human body. Instead, designers simplify the physics in even the most realistic simulations. For Mario games, this simplification is enhanced even more, but this is a good thing. By simplifying the physics of *Super Mario World*, the design team allowed players to focus not on mastering a finicky set of baseline mechanics but rather on larger, more engaging challenges that combine mechanics and skills in interesting ways. This is especially true for gravity in platformers; players don't need to be doing calculus all the time. *Super Mario World* accomplishes all of its design goals with two falling speeds in dry levels, and two swim/walk speeds in water levels. Intricate physics might work in some games, but they're by no means necessary, and might even be a hindrance.

Use Composite Game Design Techniques, Especially When Working on Mechanics

The basic idea behind a composite game is framed by the question, "How does the player use the mechanics/skills of genre X to solve the problems of genre Y?" In *Super Mario World*, it's about how Mario uses platforming skills and mechanics to solve action problems, and vice versa. That vice versa is pretty important because it's responsible for the back-and-forth flow between declensions. The four skill themes all show how momentum, reflexes, precision, and timing can solve a variety of both platforming and action problems. It's not hard to see how this could extend to other games, but combining genres is the easy part. The hard part is figuring out if there's another division like timing/speed that works for the mechanics you're interested in. To some degree, steps four and five will help figure out that problem. The next two design lessons will also help with the most important thing: always move back and forth between composited genres. That back-and-forth rhythm is what makes composite games so enjoyable. No game is perfect, but by making each level just different enough, players will be frustrated less often, and will more roundly learn the skills the game has to teach them, without even knowing that they have.

Are good games always composite games? Of course not. There are alternatives in the arcade and set-piece styles, although the latter of those two styles can overlap with composite design significantly. But if nothing else, this book should make it clear how composite design makes it easy to create novel, coherent content. It also makes it tremendously easy to organize that content and view your own content critically, as some of the other lessons will illustrate.

Iterate and Then Accumulate

All of the skill themes have one thing in common: They begin with iteration and end with accumulation. They all differ in the relative proportions and exact executions, but it's clear that this process does take place naturally. Indeed, if a designer is working on several levels based on the same core, he or she *must* iterate before accumulating. How can two ideas stack up in an accumulation if there has only been one idea?

The point of this piece of advice is to begin the design process with iteration and accumulation in mind. Every theme in every game is going to be different, and some games may not fit these principles at all. Understanding this pattern may help to make greater sense out of the games we study, the games we make, and the games we love to play.

Index

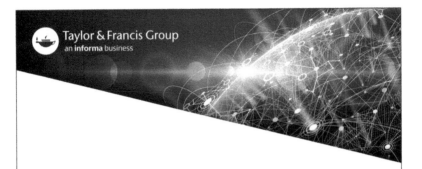

9 781138 323261